LEGENDS OF THE SUFIS

SELECTED ANECDOTES

FROM THE WORK ENTITLED

THE ACTS OF THE ADEPTS

(MENĀQIBU 'L 'ĀRIFĪN)

BY

SHEMSU-'D-DĪN AHMED, EL EFLĀKĪ

TRANSLATED BY

JAMES W. REDHOUSE

PREFACE BY
SOLOMON JAMES

AZAFRAN BOOKS

Preface by Solomon James under copyright © 2017 by Azafran Books

Published by Azafran Books –
http://www.azafranbooks.com/

ISBN-13: 978-0-9957279-4-6 (paperback)

First published: 1881 (London)
First published in this edition: September 2017

Edited, formatted & design concept by Solomon James
Cover design & design concept by B.K.

Azafran Books
info@azafranbooks.com

CONTENTS

PREFACE BY SOLOMON JAMES   p.5

TRANSLATOR'S PREFACE   p.7

SELECTED ANECDOTES

I.	Bahā'u-'d-Dīn, Veled, Sultānu-'l-'Ulemā	p.13
II.	Seyyid Burhānu-'d-Dīn, Sirr-Dān	p.25
III.	Mevlānā Jelālu-'d-Dīn, Muhammed	p.31
IV.	Shemsu-'d-Dīn, Tebrīzī	p.133
V.	Sheykh Salāhu-'d-Dīn, Ferīdūn	p.147
VI.	Chelebī Husāmu-'d-Dīn, Hasan	p.150
VII.	Bahā'u-'d-Dīn, Sultan Veled	p.161
VIII.	Chelebī Emīr 'Ārif	p.166
IX.	Genealogical	p.174

PUBLISHER'S NOTE

In presenting this edition of the 'Acts of the Adepts' it has been thought best to adhere to the spelling used by Sir James Redhouse in his translation first published in 1881. The modern equivalents will no doubt emerge in the mind of the contemporary reader. There appear also to be some discrepancies in rendering A.H. dates into A.D., and these have been kept as in the original.

PREFACE BY SOLOMON JAMES

THERE is little argument regarding Jalaluddin Rumi - often referred to as *Maulana* or *Mevlana* meaning 'Our Master' – as being one of the very greatest saints and mystics of all peoples. He was also a Master of the Way, in Sufic terminology. This book is a selection of anecdotes about the teachings of Rumi as well as his associates, family, and associates. It is an important document in the life and teachings of the Mevlevi School, as is one of the five source books generally regarded as accepted material on this tradition: the others are the *Mathnavi*, *The Divan of Shamsi-i-Tabriz*, the Letters of Rumi, and *Fihi ma Fihi*.

This collection of anecdotes often comes under the title of *Acts of the Adepts*, as was its original title in English (translated by James Redhouse). However, similar to many works of antiquity, there is no one authoritative version of this collection. Various compilations of Eflaki's work exist, in a range of languages. The book is in effect what we would call in modern parlance a hagiography. Under such circumstances there are stories, tales, and anecdotes that may seem 'unbelievable' or 'exaggerated' to a modern mind. Perhaps the reader of today should consider that such a collection functions upon several levels, and one of these may be as form of teaching material. It is well documented that Sufic materials often lend themselves as a means to test the mind and reaction of the hearer. Stories and tales taken at face value, and processed by a literal mind, may create their own obstacles in the reading. It is likely then, we must consider, that some of the contents of this collection also fare upon such levels above and beyond the literal. Other anecdotes were included, no doubt, because they were genuinely perceived to be reports of Rumi and his associates after the death of the great Master. It is a facet of human nature that tales and stories of saints and mystics are often eulogized and worshiped as 'gospel.' The reader of today should be mindful of this character flaw.

In recent years Rumi's life and work has undergone a popular revival in the western world. His work is now among the best-selling poetry of today, aided by translations that place his verse and meaning within modern verse styles. As is common among Sufic materials there is a pattern that renders them amenable to present-day terms, and which buffers them against becoming crystallized or succumbing to dogmatism. As in all human systems, there are those that are traditionalists and those that are innovators.

Legends of the Sufis, as the title suggests, contains miraculous or apparently supernatural events that appear frequently throughout. Yet the reader should bear in mind that they are not there merely to impress upon the gullible witness or to incite an emotional response. They have their purpose and function within the context of such literature. That this book, and its content, adheres to Sufic materials is without doubt. As such, it addresses a psychological aspect of the reader that many books lack. The information herewith has been available to potential readers for more than seven hundred years; still, there are those who seek to imitate its practices, such as the famous whirling dance. I can only suggest that the reader consider processing the material that they hold in their hands rather than imitating the actions of a bygone era.

Legends of the Sufis may contain everything or nothing for the modern person. As in all things, one must leave the distinction clearly at the feet of the honourable reader.

Solomon James, September 2017

TRANSLATOR'S PREFACE

THE historian El Eflākī was a disciple of Chelebī Emīr 'Ārif, a grandson of the author of the Mesnevī. 'Ārif died in A.D.1320; but as the dates of 'Ārif's successors are carried down to A.H. 754 (A.D. 1353), when Eflākī's collection of anecdotes was completed, the historian must have outlived this last date. As a disciple of the Emīr 'Ārif, he was a dervish of the order named Mevlevī, as being followers of the rule and practices of Mevlānā Jelālu-'d-Dīn, er-Rūmī, commonly known in English literature as "the dancing dervishes," expressed by Americans: "whirling dervishes." The dervishes of the order do not all dance or "whirl." Some are musicians, and some singers or chanters, who may, however, be occasional dancers also.

Eflākī's work gives a sufficiency of dates to fix the principal events that he commemorates. His dates do not agree exactly with those found in other historians. They are, however, sufficiently near for general purposes not of a chronologically critical nature. They commence with A.H. 605 A.D. (1208), and thus cover a period of 145 years dated, besides another 30 years of the lifetime of Jelāl's grandfather undated, who was a noble of such high standing and of so great a reputation for learning and sanctity at Balkh, that the king gave him his only daughter in marriage, unsolicited. His mother was also a princess of the same royal house with his wife.

This royal house was the one known in history as that of *Kh'ārezm-shāh* or the Kharezmians. They were overthrown, and Balkh (the ancient Bactra, or Zariaspa), their capital, destroyed, by Jengīz Khan in A.D. 1211. A remnant of their kingdom was continued for twelve years longer by the last of the line, who died, at once a fugitive and an invader, in Āzerbāyjān, in a battle fought against the combined forces of Egypt, Syria, and Asia Minor.

Jelāl's family claimed descent from Abū-Bekr, a father-in-law and the first successor of Muhammed, the lawgiver of Islām. One of the descendants of Abū-Bekr was among the conquerors of the ancient Bactria, when it was first brought under Muslim rule, in about A.D. 650, under the Caliph 'Uthmān and his children had maintained a prominent position in that country, possessed of great wealth, until the time immediately preceding the irruption of Jengīz.

Jelāl was the youngest of three children, two being sons, born of the princess, his mother, in Balkh. The eldest, a daughter, was already married, and remained behind with her husband, when her father and brothers left their native city some time between A.D. 1208 and 1211, in which latter year they were at Bagdād. There is no further mention of Jelāl's elder brother. Jelāl was five years old when they left Balkh. By way of Bagdād they went to Mekka, thence to Damascus, and next to Erzinjān, in Armenia; thence to Larenda, in Asia Minor. Jelāl's mother was still with the party. He was now eighteen years old; and was married, at Larenda, to a lady named Gevher (Pearl), daughter of a certain Lala Sherefu-'d-Dīn of Samarqand, in A.D. 1226.[1] She bore him two sons there, 'Alā'u-'d-Dīn (afterwards killed in a tumult at Qonya) and Bahā'u-'d-Dīn Sultān Veled, through whom the succession of the house was continued. She appears to have died rather young; for Jelāl afterwards married another lady of Qonya, who outlived him, and by whom he had two other children, a son and a daughter. (See Anecdotes, Chap. III., No. 69, for a variant.)

After the birth of Sultān Veled at Larenda, Jelāl's father was invited to Qonya by the Seljūqi king, 'Alā'u-'d-Dīn Kayqubād, where he founded a college, and where he died in A.D. 1231. The king built a marble mausoleum over his grave, with this date inscribed on it. The king himself died, five years later, in A.D. 1236.

At his father's death, Jelāl went to Aleppo and Damascus for several years to study, and then returned to Qonya, where he was appointed professor of four separate colleges. His reputation for learning and sanctity became very great.

But before this journey to Damascus, he appears to have paid a visit to Larenda. For, a former pupil of his father's at Balkh, who had become a great saint and anchoret, came to Qonya to seek Jelāl, and was the cause of his returning from Larenda to the capital.

This was the Sheykh and Seyyid Burhānu-'d-Dīn, who became Jelāl's spiritual teacher for some time. The dates given do not agree in the various branches of Eflākī's compilation; for he here gives a period of nine years spiritual study at Qonya under Burhān.

After Burhān's instructions and departure from Qonya to Qaysariyya, where he died, and after Jelāl's studies at Aleppo and Damascus, with his subsequent return to Qonya and appointment to the four colleges, another great saint came to visit Jelāl at this latter city. This was Shemsu-'d-Dīn of Tebrīz, for whom Jelāl conceived a very great friendship. He is mentioned in the Mesnevī several times in very high terms. He appears to have been exceedingly aggressive and domineering in his manner. This roused a fierce animosity against him, which at length broke out in a tumult. Jelāl's eldest son, 'Alā'u-'d-Dīn, was killed or mortally hurt in this disturbance. The local police seized Shemsu-'d-Dīn in consequence, and he was never again seen alive by his friends. Jelāl went himself to Damascus, in hopes that he might have been sent away, or have got away, privately. But the effort was fruitless. Later traditions cause his corpse to have been recovered and buried at Qonya, differing, however, as to the place of interment.

When Jelāl found that he required assistance in conducting all the various duties that fell on him, he selected first for that office his former fellow-student, Sheykh Salāhu-'d-Dīn Ferīdūn, surnamed Zer-Kūb (the Gold-beater), from his business. He assisted Jelāl for about ten years, and died in A.D. 1258.

Jelāl now took as his assistant his own favourite pupil, Hasan Husāmu-'d-Dīn, surnamed the son of Akhī-Turk, through his being descended from some man of celebrity of the name or designation of Akhī-Turk. There appears to have been a large family of very influential men residing at Qonya and other towns of Asia Minor, all calling themselves Akhī, and distinguished as Akhī: Ahmed, Akhī: Eshref, etc. The word "Akhī" is Arabic, and signifies "my brother." It may also mean "one related to a brother," as a servant, slave, client, etc., of some prince, etc.; or of some dervish "brother" of some religious order. Indeed, these very numerous individuals named Akhī, may have been each a "brother" of such a fraternity or fraternities, or even of some industrial guild.

Ten years after Husām was taken as his assistant by Jelāl, this latter was called to his rest in December A.D. 1273; and was buried in his father's mausoleum, leaving Husām as his successor. But meanwhile, at Husām's suggestion, and with himself as the first amanuensis thereof, the Mesnevī had been composed, in six volumes, books, or parts, by Jelāl. The second volume was commenced in A.D. 1263. There had been an interval of two years

between the completion of the first and this, caused by Husām's grief at the death of his wife. The whole work is stated to contain twenty-six thousand six hundred and sixty couplets. A seventh volume or book has been also attributed to the Mesnevī, to make up the number to that of the "seven planets;" some say it was composed or collected by Sultan Veled. The anecdotes of Eflākī make mention of many hundreds of odes composed also by Jelāl.

He is said to have instituted his peculiar order of dervishes, with their special dress, the Indian garb of mourning, in memory of his murdered friend, Shemsu-'d-Dīn of Tebrīz; and to have adopted the use of instrumental music, the flute, the rebeck, the drum, and the tambourine, with singing or chanting, as an accompaniment to the holy dance, on account of the lethargic nature of the "Romans." As a child is tempted to take a salutary medicine by the exhibition of a little jam or honey, so Jelāl judged that the "Romans" might be tempted to a devotional love for God through the bait of sweet sounds addressed to their outward senses. Dancing or twirling by dervishes was of much older date, as will be recollected in one of the tales of the Arabian Nights.

Husām died in A.D. 1284, just ten years after his teacher Jelāl; whose son, Bahā'u-'d-Dīn, Sultan Veled, succeeded Husām as chief of the order, and died in A.D. 1312. His son, Chelebī Emīr ʿĀrif, succeeded him, and passed away in A.D. 1320; two of his half-brothers becoming chiefs of the order after him in succession.

Eflākī informs us that he undertook the compilation of his work at the express desire of his spiritual teacher, Chelebī Emīr ʿĀrif. The preface gives the year A.H. 710 (A.D. 1310) as that of its commencement, and the colophon at the end mentions A.H.754 (A.D. 1353) as the date of its completion. He thus spent forty-three years in his labour of love. The copy used for the present translation was written in A.H. 1027 (A.D. 1617), and belongs to the library of the India Office, being No. 1670. It is a quarto volume of 291 numbered folios of two pages each folio, and twenty-three lines in each page. It is subdivided into a preface, of two folios, and ten chapters of very different lengths.

The work contains many hundreds of anecdotes, related to Eflākī by trustworthy reporters, whose names are generally given, and a few for which he vouches himself as an eyewitness. Every anecdote is the account of a miracle wrought by the living or the dead; or is the narrative of some strange or striking event. It is, in fact, a species of the Acts of the Apostles of the Mevlevi dervish fathers, and is a rare specimen of what fervid religious enthusiasm can invent or exaggerate, pious credulity can believe, and confiding ignorance accept. In these days of Christian "Spiritualism," let not the reader be over-shocked at learning that Muslim "Saints," lovers of their Creator, and beloved by Him in return, hold themselves and are held by their dervish brethren to be the successors and spiritual inheritors of the prophets, from Adam to Muhammed; that, in virtue of this spiritual communion with God, they know all the secrets and mysteries of heaven and earth, and not only suspend or overrule the laws of nature at their will, but also deal out death or disease by their anger, health or prosperity by their blessing; the whole in strict accordance, however, with the eternal will and foreknowledge of Him by whom alone all things are made.

The anecdotes translated are chosen as being characteristic of various points of dervish credence or assertion. Most of them inculcate some moral truth or point of practical wisdom. A few will be found, however, to go far beyond the credible; and one or two, unless totally misunderstood by the translator, are simply and grossly blasphemous. These last are here given as specimens of the exaggerated dervish doctrines which cause the orthodox among the 'Ulemā[2] of Islām to hold all such quasi-religious associations to be more or less heterodox.

The dervishes of Islām appear to be a kind of Gnostics. They style themselves Poor, Impassioned, Adepts, and Perfect. In many respects their doctrines correspond with those of Buddha, Pythagoras, and Plato, making all souls that are destined to salvation to be emanations from the divine Light or Glory of God, in which they will be again congregated; and all those doomed to perdition to have been formed out of the Fire of His wrath, to which also they will eventually be consigned.

It is but too patent to the translator that he is bound to sue for the kind indulgence of a critical public, in offering them the present volume in verse. He has no claim to being a poet himself; and had never practised the art of metrical composition until very lately. Sensible himself to the earnestness of thought and beauty of diction imbedded in the writings of the great poets of Islam, and keenly aware of the condition of dry bones to which literal prose translation almost always reduces a songster's numbers, he has preferred to clothe his author in a presentable garb, though it be but a crumpled wrap, rather than exhibit him to readers of taste as a mangled mass, stripped of all beauty, and in great measure divested even of cognisable form, through the conflict of dictions and diversities of ideas.

He is in the position of the raindrop sung by Sa'dī (see Chap. III., No. 14., of the Anecdotes), and mentioned of old by Chardin, Addison, and Sir William Jones. May the thoughts in the Mesnevī be the gems that will make his effort acceptable to the British public. At most, he is but the diver who risks extinction in the hope that he may have a chance to offer an acceptable pearl of price to those for whom he has worked

"A raindrop, from a cloud distilled,
At sea's expanse with tremor filled,
Mused: 'Where the main rolls, am I aught?
In ocean's presence, sure, I'm naught.'
Itself, thus eyed with scorn profound,
In oyster's bosom nurture found.
Time's wheel wrought changes manifold;
Rich pearl of price the raindrop's told.
Meek modesty its prize received;
By naught's gate ent'ring, worth achieved."

KILBURN PRIORY, LONDON. 1880.

Footnotes

1. He must have been born in about A.D. 1204 or 1205, to have been five years old when the family left Balkh. In 1226 he would, therefore, be twenty-one or twenty-two years of age.
2. The "*Ulemā of Islām*" are *the Learned* Doctors of Law and Divinity; their chief is the Lord Chancellor. They are ignorantly spoken of as "*priests*" and "*clergy*" by Europeans. There are no "*priests*" in Islām. The 'Ulemā may be likened to the Jewish Rabbis. They often have followed, and do follow, all kinds of trades.

CHAPTER I

Bahā'u-'d-Dīn, Veled, Sultānu-'l-'Ulemā (The Beauty of the Religion of Islam, Son, Sultan of the Doctors of the Law).

1.

THE king of Khurāsān, (1) 'Alā'u-'d-Dīn Muhammed, Khurrem-Shāh, uncle of Jelālu-'d-Dīn Muhammed Kh'ārezm-Shāh, and the proudest, as he was the most handsome man of his time, gave his daughter, Melika'i-Jihān (Queen of the World), as to the only man worthy of her, to Jelālu-'d-Dīn Huseyn, el Khatībī, of the race of Abū-Bekr.

An ancestor of his was one of the original Muslim conquerors of Khurāsān. He was himself very virtuous and learned, surrounded with numerous disciples. He had not married until then; which gave him many an anxious and self-accusing thought.

He himself, the king, the king's daughter, and the king's Vazīr were all four warned in a dream by the Prince of the Apostles of God (Muhammed) that he should wed the princess; which was done. He was then thirty years old. In due course, nine months afterwards, a son was born to him, and was named Bahā'u-'d-Dīn Muhammed. He is commonly mentioned as Bahā'u-'d-Dīn Veled.

When adolescent, this latter was so extremely learned that the family of his mother wished to raise him to the throne as king; but this he utterly rejected.

By the divine command, as conveyed in the selfsame night, and in an identical dream, to three hundred of the most learned men of

the city of Balkh, (2) the capital of the kingdom, where he dwelt, those sage doctors unanimously conferred upon him the honorific title of Sultānu-'l-'Ulemā, and they all became his disciples.

Such are the names and titles by which he is more commonly mentioned; but he is also styled Mevlānāyi Buzurg (the Greater or Elder Master). Many miracles and prodigies were attributed to him; and some men were found who conceived a jealousy at his growing reputation and influence.

2.

In A.H. 605 (A.D. 1208) he, Bahā'u-'d-Dīn Veled, began to preach against the innovations of the king and sundry of his courtiers, declaiming against the philosophers and rationalists, while he pressed all his hearers to study and practise the precepts of Islām. Those courtiers maligned him with the king, calling him an intriguer who had designs on the throne. The king sent and made him an offer of the sovereignty, promising to retire elsewhere himself. Bahā answered that he had no concern with earthly greatness, being a poor recluse; and that he would willingly leave the country, so as to remove from the king's mind all misgivings on his score.

He accordingly quitted Balkh, with a suite of about forty souls, after delivering a public address in the great mosque before the king and people. In this address he foretold the advent of the Moguls to overturn the kingdom, possess the country, destroy Balkh, and drive out the king, who would then flee to the Roman land, and there at length be killed.

So he left Balkh, as the prophet (Muhammed) had fled from Mekka to Medīna. His son Jelālu-'d-Dīn was then five, and the elder brother, 'Alā'u-'d-Dīn, seven years old.

The people everywhere on his road, hearing of his approach or forewarned in dreams of his coming, flocked to meet him and do him honour. Thus he drew near to Bagdād. Here he was met by the great Sheykh Shahābu-'d-Dīn, 'Umer, Suherverdī, the most eminent man of the place, deputed by the Caliph Musta'zim to do him honour. He became the guest of the Sheykh.

The Caliph sent him a present of three thousand sequins, but he declined the gift as being money unlawfully acquired. He also refused to visit the Caliph; but consented to preach in the great mosque after the noon service of worship on the following Friday, the Caliph being present. In his discourse he reproached the Caliph to his face with his evil course of life, and warned him of his approaching slaughter by the Moguls with great cruelty and ignominy. The Caliph again sent him rich presents in money, horses, and valuables, but he refused to accept them.

Before Bahā'u-'d-Dīn quitted Bagdād, intelligence was received there of the siege of Balkh, of its capture, and of its entire destruction, with its twelve thousand mosques, by the Mogul army of five hundred thousand men commanded by Jengīz in person (in A.H. 608, A.D. 1211). Fourteen thousand copies of the Qur'ān were destroyed, fifteen thousand students and professors of the law were slain, and two hundred thousand adult male inhabitants led out and shot to death with arrows.

Bahā'u-'d-Dīn went from Bagdād to Mekka, (3) performed the greater pilgrimage there, proceeding thence to Damascus, and next to Malatia (Melitene, on the Upper Euphrates), where, in A.H. 614 (A.D. 1217), he heard of the death of Jengīz. The Seljūqī Sultan, 'Alā'u-'d-Dīn Keyqubād, was then sovereign of the land of Rome (Rūm, *i.e.*, Asia Minor), and was residing at Sīwās (Sebaste). In A.H. 620 (A.D. 1223) Sultan Jelālu-'d-Dīn, the dispossessed monarch of Kh'ārezm (Chorasmia) was killed in a battle fought by him in Azerbāyjān (Atropatene) against the Sultans of Rome, Syria, and Egypt, when his forces were totally defeated. And thus ended that great dynasty, after ruling about a hundred and forty years.

Bahā'u-'d-Dīn went from Malatia and remained four years near Erzinjān (the ancient Aziris, on the Western Euphrates), in Armenia, at a college built for him by a saintly lady, 'Ismet Khātūn. She was the wife of the local sovereign, Melik Fakhru-'d-Dīn. She and her husband both died, and then Bahā'u-'d-Dīn passed on to Larenda (in Cataonia), in Asia Minor, and remained there about seven years at the head of a college, the princess Melika'i-Jihān, his mother, being still with him.

Here it was that his younger son, Jelālu-'d-Dīn Muhammed, the future author of the Mesnevī, attained to man's estate, being then eighteen years old; when, in A.H. 623 (A.D. 1226), he married a young lady named Gevher Khātūn, daughter of the Lala Sherefu-'d-Dīn, of Samarqand. She gave birth in due course to Jelāl's eldest son, 'Alā'u-'d-Dīn.

The king had now returned to his capital, Qonya (the ancient Iconium). Hearing of Bahā'u-'d-Dīn's great learning and sanctity, the king sent and invited him to the capital, where he installed him in a college, and soon professed himself a disciple. Many miracles are related as having been worked at Qonya by Bahā'u-'d-Dīn, who at length died there on Friday, the 18th of Rebī'u-'l-ākhir, A.H. 628 (February A.D. 1231). The Sultan erected a marble mausoleum over his tomb, on which this date is recorded. Many miracles continued to occur at this sanctuary. The Sultan died also a few years later, in A.H. 634 (A.D. 1236).

(After the death of Bahā'u-'d-Dīn Veled, and the acquisition of still greater fame by his son Jelālu-'d-Dīn, who received the honorific title of Khudāvendgār—*Lord*—the father was distinguished from the son, among the disciples, by the customary title of Mevlānā Buzurg—*the Greater or Elder Master.* The traditions collected by Eflākī, relating to this period, vary considerably from one another on minor points of date and order of succession, though the main facts come out sufficiently clear.)

3.

Jelāl's son, Sultan Veled, related to Eflākī that his father Jelāl used frequently to say, "I and all my disciples will be under the protection of the *Great Master*, my father, on the day of resurrection; and under His guidance we shall enter the divine presence; God will pardon all of us for His sake."

4.

It is related that when the *Great Master* departed this life, his son, Jelālu-'d-Dīn, was fourteen years old. (This is apparently a copyist's error for "twenty-four." Jalāl is said to have been born in A.H. 604—A.D. 1207.) He married when seventeen (or eighteen); and often did he say in the presence of the congregation of his friends, "The *Great Master* will remain with me a few years. I shall be in need of Shemsu-'d-Dīn of Tebrīz (the capital of Azerbāyjān); for every prophet has had an Abū-Bekr, as Jesus had His apostles."

5.

Shortly after the death of the Great Master Bahā'u-'d-Dīn Veled, news was received by the Sultan 'Alā'u-'d-Dīn of Qonya of the arrival of Sultan Jelālu-'d-Dīn Kh'ārezm-Shāh on the borders of Asia Minor. The Sultan went and prayed at the tomb of the deceased saint, and then prepared to meet the Kh'ārezmians, who were in the neighbourhood of Erzenu-'r-Rūm (Erzen of the Romans, the ancient Arzes, now Erzerum). Scouts brought in the intelligence that the Kh'ārezmians were very numerous; and great anxiety prevailed among the Sultan's troops. He resolved to see for himself.

He put on a disguise and set out with a few followers, on fleet horses, for the Kh'ārezmian camp. They gave out that they were nomad Turks of the neighbourhood, their ancestors having come from the Oxus; that latterly the Sultan had withdrawn his favour from them; and that, in consequence, they had for some time past been looking for the Kh'ārezmian advent. This was reported to

the king, Jelālu-'d-Dīn, who sent for them and received them kindly, giving them tents and assigning them rations.

During the night King Jelālu-'d-Dīn began to reflect that every one had hitherto spoken well of Sultan 'Alā'u-'d-Dīn, and a doubt arose in his mind in consequence respecting the story of these newcomers, especially as he learned that the Sultan was on his march to meet him. Consulting with the Prince of Erzenu-'r-Ram, further perquisition was postponed until the morrow.

But at midnight the deceased saint of Qonya, Bahā-Veled, appeared in a dream to Sultan 'Alā'u-'d-Dīn, and warned him to fly at once. The Sultan awoke, found it was a dream, and went to sleep again. The saint now appeared a second time. The Sultan saw himself seated on his throne, and the saint coming to him, smiting him on the breast with his staff, and angrily saying, "Why sleepest thou? Arise!"

Now the Sultan did arise, quietly called his people, saddled horses, and stole away out of the camp. Towards morning King Jelāl caused guards to be placed round the tents of the strangers to watch them. But afterwards, when orders were given to bring them to the king's presence to be questioned, their tents were found to be empty. Pursuit was attempted, but in vain.

After an interval the two armies came into collision. The Sultan of Qonya was victorious. From that time forward, whenever difficulties threatened, he always betook himself to the shrine of the saint, Bahā Veled, who always answered his prayers.

(As Sultan Jelālu-'d-Dīn Kh'ārezm-Shāh has already been stated to have died in battle in Azerbāyjān in A.D. 1223, whereas the saint of Qonya did not die until A.D. 1231, eight years afterwards, the discrepancy of that date with the present anecdote is irreconcilable.)

6.

The Great Master, Bahā Veled, used to say that while he himself lived no other teacher would be his equal, but that when his son, Jelālu-'d-Dīn, should succeed him at his death, that son of his would equal and even surpass him:

7.

Seyyid Burhānu-'d-Dīn Termīzī (4) is related to have said that one night the door of the mausoleum of Bahā Veled opened of itself, and that a great glory shone forth from it, which gradually filled his house, so that no shadow fell from anything. The glory then gradually filled the city in like manner, spreading thence over the whole face of nature. On beholding this prodigy the Seyyid swooned away.

This vision is a sure indication that the whole human race will one day own themselves the disciples of the descendants of the great saint.

8.

Before he quitted Balkh, Bahā Veled one day saw a man performing his devotions in the great mosque in his shirt sleeves, with his coat upon his back. Bahā reproved him, telling him to put

on his coat properly and decently, then to continue his devotions. "And what if I will not?" asked the man in a disdainful tone. "Thy dead-like soul will obey my command, quit thy body, and thou wilt die!" answered Bahā. Instantly the man fell dead; and crowds flocked to become disciples to the saint who spoke with such power and authority.

9.

When Sultan 'Alā'u-'d-Dīn had fortified Qonya, he invited Bahā Veled to mount to the terraced roof of the palace, thence to survey the walls and towers. After his inspection, Bahā remarked to the Sultan, "Against torrents, and against the horsemen of the enemy, thou hast raised a goodly defence. But what protection hast thou built against those unseen arrows, the sighs and moans of the oppressed, which overleap a thousand walls and sweep whole worlds to destruction? Go to, now! Strive to acquire the blessings of thy subjects. These are a stronghold, compared to which the walls and turrets of the strongest castles are as nothing."

10.

On one occasion Sultan 'Alā'u-'d-Dīn paid a visit to Bahā Veled. In lieu of his hand the latter offered the tip of his staff to be kissed by the Sultan, who thought within himself: "The proud scholar!" Bahā read the Sultan's thoughts as a seer, and remarked in reply thereto: "Mendicant students are bound to be humble and lowly. Not so a Sultan of the Faith who has attained to the utmost circumference of the orbit thereof, and revolves therein."

11.

A certain Sheykh Hajjāj, a disciple of Bahā Veled and one of God's elect not known to the herd of mankind, quitted the college after the decease of his teacher, and betook himself to his former trade of a weaver, therewith to gain an honest livelihood. He used to buy the coarsest brown bread of unsifted flour, mash this up with water, and break his fast with this sop alone. All the rest of his earnings he saved up until they would reach to two or three hundred piastres. This sum he would then carry to the college, and place it in the shoes of his teacher's son, Jelālu-'d-Dīn, the new rector. This practice he continued so long as he lived.

At his death a professional washer was appointed to perform the last ablution for Sheykh Hajjāj. In the execution of his office the washer was about to touch the privities of the deceased, when the defunct seized his hand with so strong a grip as to make him scream with pain and fright. The friends came to rescue him, but they were unable to release the imprisoned hand. They therefore sent word to Jelālu-'d-Dīn of what had occurred. He came and saw, knew the reason, and whispered into the ear of the deceased man: "The poor simpleton has been unaware of the high station of thy sanctity. Pardon his unintentional transgression for my sake." Immediately the poor washer's hand was released; but three days afterwards he was himself washed and borne lifeless to his grave.

12.

The Sultan had a governor of his childhood still living, the Emīr Bedru-'d-Dīn Guhertāsh, commonly known as the Dizdār

(Castellan), whom he held in great esteem. One day, as Bahā Veled was lecturing in the mosque, in presence of the Sultan and his court, he suddenly called upon the Dizdār to recite any ten verses of the Qur'ān, saying he would then expound them to the congregation. The Dizdār had been admiring the eloquence of the preacher's expositions. Upon this sudden call, without the slightest hesitation and without ever having committed them to memory, he recited the first ten verses of chapter xxiii., "The believers have attained to prosperity," etc., which Bahā forthwith explained in such a manner as to draw down the plaudits of the assembly. The Dizdār, with the Sultan's permission, went to the foot of the pulpit and declared himself a disciple to Bahā. "Then," said the preacher, "as a thank-offering for this happy event, do thou build and endow a college where my descendants shall teach their disciples after me." The Dizdār did so, and richly endowed it. This is the college where Jelālu-'d-Dīn afterwards lived. When the Dizdār died he left all his possessions to enrich the foundation. (See chap. III. No. 69.)

13.

The Sultan had a dream (something like one of Nebuchadnezzar's). He saw himself with a head of gold, a breast of silver, a belly of brass, thighs of lead, and shanks of tin. Bahā Veled explained the dream as follows:—"All will go well in the kingdom during thy lifetime. It will be as silver in the days of thy son; as brass in the next generation, when the rabble will get the upper hand. Troubles will thicken during the next reign; and after that the kingdom of Rome will go to ruin, the house of Seljūq will

come to an end, and unknown upstarts will seize the reins of government."

Footnotes

1. Eastern Persia.
2. The ancient *Bactra*, sometimes called *Zariaspa*, the capital of Bactria.
3. Incorrectly written Mecca by Europeans.
4. Of Termīz (Tirmez), on the north bank of the Oxus, near to Balkh.

CHAPTER II

Seyyid Burhānu-'d-Dīn, Sirr-Dān, el Muhaqqiq, el Huseynī, of the posterity of Yā-Sīn (Muhammed). (1)

(HE is called Seyyid, the *"Syud"* of our East India authorities, for the reason that he was a descendant of the prophet, of whom Yā-Sīn is one of the titles, as it is also the name of the thirty-sixth chapter of the Qur'ān, at the head of which the two letters stand which form the name. Burhānu-'d-Dīn means *The Proof of the Religion;* Sirr-Dān signifies *The Confidant,* one who possesses a knowledge of a secret or secrets, a mystery or mysteries. Muhaqqiq is one who verifies, who probes the truth; and Huseynī indicates that the Seyyid was of the branch of Huseyn, the younger of the two sons of Fātima, Muhammed's only child that left posterity.)

1.

Seyyid Burhānu-'d-Dīn was popularly known by the name of Sirr-Dān at Balkh, Bukhārā, (Alexandria Oxiana?), and Termīz. His discourse was continually running upon the subjects of spiritual and mental phenomena, of the mysteries of earth and of heaven.

When Bahā Veled quitted Balkh, the Seyyid went to Termīz, and there secluded himself as a hermit. After a while again he began to lecture in public on the significations of knowledge. Suddenly, one morning, that of Friday the 18th of Rebī'u-'l-ākhir, A.H. 628 (February, 1231 A.D.), he cried out most bitterly, in a flood of tears, "Alas! My master has passed away from this tabernacle of dust to the abode of sincerity!" His words and the date were noted down, and, on inquiry, after his arrival in Qonya, were found to correspond exactly with the moment of Bahā Veled's decease.

2.

For forty days the disciples at Termīz mourned for the death of the great teacher. At the end of that period the Seyyid said: "The son of my master, his successor, Jelālu-'d-Dīn Muhammed, is left alone and is wishing to see me. I must go to the land of Rome and place myself at his service, delivering over to him the trust which my teacher confided to my safe-keeping."

3.

When the Seyyid reached Qonya, Bahā Veled had been dead about a year, and Jelāl had gone to Larenda. The Seyyid applied himself for several months to devotional seclusion in one of the mosques of Qonya; after which he sent off a letter to Jelāl by the hands of two mendicants, saying: "Come and meet this stranger to thee at the resting-place of thy father, for Larenda is not a place of permanency for thee. From that hill (on which Bahā's mausoleum was built) a fire will shower down on the city of Qonya."

After reading this epistle Jelāl returned to Qonya with all possible despatch. There he went at once to visit the Seyyid, who came forth from the mosque to receive him. They embraced. They now entered into conversation on various subjects. So delighted was the Seyyid with the expositions set forth by Jelāl that he kissed the soles of his feet, and exclaimed: "A hundredfold hast thou surpassed thy father in all knowledge of the humanities; but thy father was versed also in the mysteries of mute reality and ecstasy. From this day forward my desire is that thou shouldest also acquire that knowledge,—the knowledge possessed by the prophets and the saints, which is entitled *The Science of Divine Intuition*—the science spoken of by God (in Qur'ān xviii. 64): 'We have taught him a science from within us.' This knowledge did I acquire from my teacher; do thou receive it from me, so that thou mayest be the heir to thy father in spiritual matters as well as in things temporal. Thou wilt then be his second self."

Jelāl complied with all the Seyyid pressed upon him. He took the Seyyid to his college, and for nine years received instruction from him. Some accounts make it appear that Jelāl first became the Seyyid's disciple at this time; but others go to show that Bahā Veled gave Jelāl as a pupil to the Seyyid at Balkh, and that the Seyyid used now and then to carry Jelāl about on his shoulders, like as is practised by the nursing-tutors—*lala*—of children. (Compare chap. III., Nos. 6 and 8.)

4.

Husāmu-'d-Dīn told us that Jelāl had informed him of the following occurrence:—

The Seyyid once arrived at a certain city in Khurāsān named Sāmānek. The chief people went forth to meet him and show him honour, all excepting the Sheykhu-'l-Islām of the place (the local vice-chancellor). Nevertheless the Seyyid went to pay his respects to the legal functionary. The latter went barefoot to the door of

the house to meet the Seyyid, whose hand he kissed, and to whom he offered excuses for his seeming lack of courtesy.

In reply, the Seyyid said to him: "I am come to inform you that, on the 10th day of next month, Ramazān, you will have occasion to go forth to a hot-bath. On your way thither you will be assassinated by the emissaries of the *Old Man of the Mountain*. This I communicate to thee, that thou mayest set thy affairs in order, and repent thee of thy sins."

The Sheykhu-'l-Islām fell at the Seyyid's feet, wailing; but the latter remarked: "This is of no avail. Events are in God's hands, and He has so ordered it. Still, as thou showest so much contrition, I may add, for thy consolation, that thou wilt die in the faith, and shalt not be cut off from the divine mercy and grace."

And so it happened as thus predicted. The assassins took his life on the very day foretold by the Seyyid.

(The stronghold, Alamūt, of the *Old Man of the Mountain*, was stormed by forces sent against it by Helagū, grandson of Jengīz, in about the year A.H. 654 (A.D. 1256). The last prince of the dynasty was sent to China, and there put to death by the emperor; and thus these detestable scourges of humanity were at length suppressed.)

5.

After a certain time the Seyyid asked permission of Jelāl to go for a while to Qaysariyya (Cæsarea), but Jelāl could not spare him. So he remained at Qonya still.

Somewhat later a party of friends took the Seyyid out for a ride among the vineyards. The thought occurred to him that, without saying anything to anybody, he might now easily abscond and get away to Qaysariyya. Scarcely had he conceived this vagabond idea than his beast reared with him, threw him, and broke his leg. His friends raised him, set him again on his horse, and conducted him to a neighbouring country-house to which Jelāl had also come.

On seeing Jelāl the Seyyid exclaimed to him, "Is this the proper way to reward your teacher—to break his leg?" Jelāl at once ordered the Seyyid's boot to be removed, and saw that his foot and toes were crushed. He now passed his hands along the injured limb and blew on it. The limb was at once restored whole. Jelāl now granted permission, and the Seyyid forthwith proceeded to Qaysariyya.

6.

When the time was come that the Seyyid should die, he told his servant to prepare for him an ewer of warm water, and to go. The water was made ready, placed in the Seyyid's room, and the servant went forth. The Seyyid called after him: "Go and proclaim that the stranger Seyyid has departed to the other world." He then bolted the door, that none should enter to him.

The servant, however, had his curiosity excited by those words, and went back to the door, to listen and to see what might happen. Through a chink he saw his master perform an ablution, arrange his dress, lie down on his couch, and cry out: "All ye angels, saints, and heavens, who have at any time intrusted to me

a secret, come to me now and receive back your charges. Ye are here all present."

He then recited the following hymn:—

"God, my beloved, darling God, adored, to me incline;
My soul receive; intoxicate, release poor me distraught.
In Thee alone my heart finds peace; it fire with love divine;
Take it unto Thyself; to it both worlds are naught."

These were the Seyyid's last words, ere he yielded up his spirit. The servant carried the news to the Seyyid's friends, who gathered together, carried him forth, and buried him.

A mausoleum was raised over his grave by a rich and powerful disciple. The departed saint would not allow a cupola to stand. Twice the dome was shaken down by earthquakes, and in a dream the Seyyid himself forbade its third edification.

After the usual forty days of mourning, a letter was sent to Jelāl, who at once journeyed from Qonya to Qaysariyya, and prayed at the tomb of his deceased teacher, returning home again afterwards.

Footnotes

1. The two letters *Yā* and *Sīn* heading the thirty-sixth chapter of the Qur'ān are said to stand for the words, Yā insān, O *man!* as Mohammed is there addressed.

CHAPTER III

Mevlānā Jelālu-'d-Dīn Muhammed, the Revered Mystery of God upon Earth. (1)

JELĀLU-'D-DĪN is related to have been born at Balkh on the 6th of Rebī'u-'l-evvel, A.H. 604 (29th September 1207).

When five years old, he used at times to become extremely uneasy and restless, so much so that his attendants used to take him into the midst of themselves.

The cause of these perturbations was that spiritual forms and shapes of the absent (invisible world) would arise before his sight, that is, angelic messengers, righteous genii, and saintly men—the concealed ones of the bowers of the True One (spiritual spouses of God), used to appear to him in bodily shape, exactly as the cherubim and seraphim used to show themselves to the holy apostle of God, Muhammed, in the earlier days, before his call to the prophetic office; as Gabriel appeared to Mary, and as the four angels were seen by Abraham and Lot; as well as others to other prophets.

His father, Bahā'u-'d-Dīn Veled, the Sultānu-'l-'Ulemā, used on these occasions to coax and soothe him by saying: "These are the Occult Existences. They come to present themselves before you, to offer unto you gifts and presents from the invisible world."

These ecstasies and transports of his began to be publicly known and talked about; and the affectionately honorific title of Khudāvendgār, by which he is so often mentioned, was conferred upon him at this time by his father, who used to address him and speak of him by this title, as "My Lord."

2.

His son, Sultan Veled, related that there was a paper in the handwriting of his father, Bahā Veled, which set forth that at Balkh, when Jelāl was six years old, he was taking the air one Friday, on the terraced roof of the house, and reciting the Qur'ān, when some other children of good families came in and joined him there.

After a time, one of these children proposed that they should try and jump from thence on to a neighbouring terrace, and should lay wagers on the result.

Jelāl smiled at this childish proposal, and remarked: "My brethren, to jump from terrace to terrace is an act well adapted for cats, dogs, and the like, to perform; but is it not degrading to man, whose station is so superior? Come now, if you feel disposed, let us spring up to the firmament, and visit the regions of God's realm." As he yet spake, he vanished from their sight.

Frightened at Jelāl's sudden disappearance, the other children raised a shout of dismay, that some one should come to their assistance; when lo, in an instant, there he was again in their midst; but with an altered expression of countenance and blanched cheeks. They all uncovered before him, fell to the earth in humility, and all declared themselves his disciples.

He now told them that, as he was yet speaking to them, a company of visible forms, clad in green raiment, had led him away from them, and had conducted him about the various concentric orbs of the spheres, and through the signs of the Zodiac, showing him the wonders of the world of spirits, and bringing him back to them so soon as their cries had reached his ears.

At that age, he was used not to break his fast more often than once in three or four, and sometimes even seven, days.

3.

A different witness, a disciple of Jelāl's father, related that Bahā Veled frequently affirmed publicly that his Lord, Jelāl, was of exalted descent, being of the lineage of a king, and also of an hereditary saint.

His maternal grandmother was a daughter of the great Imām Es-Sarakhsī (2)(died at Damascus A.H. 571, A.D. 1175), who was of the lineage of the Prophet. The mother of Es-Sarakhsī was descended from the Caliph 'Alī; and Jelāl's paternal grandmother was a daughter of the King of Kh'ārezm, who resided at Balkh.

Jelāl's paternal great-great-grandmother, also, the mother of Ahmed, El-Khatībī, grandfather of Jelāl's father, was a daughter of a king of Balkh. These particulars establish that Jelāl was well descended on both sides, in a mundane and in a spiritual sense. The well-known proverb—

"Hereditary disposition ever insinuates itself,"

proved fully true in his most illustrious case.

4.

When Jelāl was seven years old, he used every morning to recite the very short chapter, cviii., of the Qur'ān—

"Verily we have given unto thee the abounding good. Therefore, do thou perform thy devotions unto thy Lord, and slaughter victims. Verily, he who evil entreateth thee is one who shall leave no issue after him."

He used to weep as he recited these inspired words.

Suddenly, God one day vouchsafed to appear to him visibly. On this he fainted away. Regaining consciousness, he heard a voice from heaven, that said—

"O Jelālu-'d-Dīn (3) By the majesty (jelāl) of Our glory, do thou henceforward cease to combat with thyself; for We have exalted thee to the station of ocular vision."

Jelāl vowed, therefore, out of gratitude for this mark of grace, to serve the Lord to the end of his days, to the utmost of his power; in the firm hope that they who followed him would also attain to that high grade of favour and excellence.

5.

Two years after the death of his father, Jelāl went from Qonya to Haleb (Aleppo) to study. (This account is altogether subversive, as to time and date, of that already given in chap. II. No. 3.)

As he was known to be a son of Bahā'u-'d-Dīn Veled, and was also an apt scholar, his professor showed him every attention.

Others were offended, and evinced their jealousy at the preference thus accorded to him. They complained to the governor of the city that Jelāl was immoral, as he was in the habit, each night, of quitting his cell at midnight for some unknown purpose. The governor resolved to see and judge for himself. He therefore hid himself in the porter's room.

At midnight, Jelāl came forth from his room, and went straight to the locked gate of the college, watched by the governor. The gate flew open; and Jelāl, followed at a distance by the governor, went through the streets to the locked city gate. This, too, opened of itself; and again both passed forth.

They went on and came to the tomb of Abraham (at Hebron, about 350 miles distant), the "Friend of the All-Merciful." There a domed edifice was seen, filled with a large company of forms in green raiment, who came forth to meet Jelāl, and conducted him into the building.

The governor hereupon lost his senses through fright, and did not recover until after the sun had risen.

Now, he could see nothing of a domed edifice, nor one single human being. He wandered about on a trackless plain for three days and three nights, hungry, thirsty, and footsore. At length he sank under his sufferings.

Meanwhile, the porter of the college had given intelligence of the governor's pursuit after Jelāl. When his officers found that he did not return, they sent a numerous party of guards to seek him. These, on the second day, met Jelāl. He told them where they

would find their master. The next day, late, they came up with him, found him to be nearly dead, and brought him home.

The governor became a sincere convert, and a disciple to Jelāl for ever after.

(A parallel tale is told of Jelāl's fetching water from the Tigris for his father by night when he was a little child at Bagdad. There, too, all the gates opened to him of themselves.)

6.

It is related that the Seyyid Burhānu-'d-Dīn was often heard to narrate that, when Jelāl was a child, the Seyyid was his governor and tutor. He had often taken Jelāl up on his shoulder, and so carried him to the empyrean. "But now," he would add, "Jelāl has attained to such eminence of station that he carries me up." These sayings of the Seyyid were repeated to Jelāl, who confirmed them with the remark: "It is quite true; and a hundredfold more also; the services rendered to me by that man are infinite."

7.

When Jelāl went to Damascus to study, he passed by Sīs in Upper Cilicia. There, in a cave, dwelt forty Christian monks, who had a great reputation for sanctity, but in reality were mere jugglers.

On the approach of Jelāl's caravan to the cave, the monks caused a little boy to ascend into the air, and there remain standing between heaven and earth.

Jelāl noticed this exhibition, and fell into a reverie. Hereupon, the child began to weep and wail, saying that the man in the reverie was frightening him. The monks told him not to be afraid, but to come down. "Oh!" cried the child, "I am as though nailed here, unable to move hand or foot."

The monks became alarmed. They flocked around Jelāl, and begged him to release the child. After a time, he seemed to hear and understand them. His answer was: "Only through the acceptance of Islām by yourselves, all of you, as well as by the child, can he be saved."

In the end they all embraced Islām, and wished to follow Jelāl as his disciples. He recommended them, however, to remain in their cave, as before, to cease from practising jugglery, and to serve God in the spirit and in truth. So he proceeded on his journey.

8.

Jelāl remained seven years, or four years, at Damascus; and there he first saw his great friend Shemsu-'d-Dīn of Tebrīz, clothed in his noted black felt and peculiar cap. Shems addressed him; but he turned away, and mixed in the crowd. Soon afterwards, he returned to Qonya by way of Qaysariyya. At this latter place, under the guiding supervision of his spiritual teacher, the Seyyid Burhānu-'d-Dīn, Jelāl fasted three consecutive periods of forty days each, (4) with only a pot of water and two or three loaves of barley bread. He showed no signs of suffering. Burhān now pronounced him perfect in all science, patent and occult, human and spiritual. (Compare chap. II. No. 3.)

9.

In the year A.H. 642 (A.D. 1244), Shemsu-'d-Dīn of Tebrīz came to Qonya.

This great man, after acquiring a reputation of superior sanctity at Tebrīz, as the disciple of a certain holy man, a basket-maker by trade, had travelled about much in various lands, in search of the best spiritual teachers, thus gaining the nickname of Perenda (the *Flier*, *Bird*, etc.).

He prayed to God that it might be revealed to him who was the most occult of the favourites of the divine will, so that he might go to him and learn still more of the mysteries of divine love.

The son of Bahā'u-'d-Dīn Veled, of Balkh, was designated to him as the man most in favour with God. Shems went, accordingly, to Qonya; arriving there on Saturday, the 26th of Jemādà-'l-ākhir, A.H. 642 (December A.D. 1244). He engaged a lodging at an inn, and pretended to be a great merchant. In his room, however, there was nothing but a broken water-pot, an old mat, and a bolster of unbaked clay. He broke his fast once in every ten or twelve days, with a damper soaked in broth of sheep's trotters.

One day, as he was seated at the gate of the inn, Jelāl came by, riding on a mule, in the midst of a crowd of students and disciples on foot.

Shemsu-'d-Dīn arose, advanced, and took hold of the mule's bridle, addressing Jelāl in these words: "Exchanger of the current coins of recondite significations, who knowest the names of the

Lord! Tell me: Was Muhammed the greater servant of God, or Bāyezīd of Bestām?"

Jelāl answered him: "Muhammed was incomparably the greater— the greatest of all prophets and all saints."

"Then," rejoined Shemsu-'d-Dīn, "how is it that Muhammed said: 'We have not known Thee, O God, as Thou rightly shouldest be known,' whereas Bāyezīd said: 'Glory unto me! How very great is my glory'?"

On hearing this question, Jelāl fainted away. On recovering his consciousness, he took his new acquaintance home with him. They were closeted together for weeks or months in holy communications.

Jelāl's disciples at length became impatient, raising a fearful and threatening tumult; so that, on Thursday, the 21st of Shewwāl, A.H. 643 (March A.D. 1246), Shemsu-'d-Dīn mysteriously disappeared; and Jelāl adopted, as a sign of mourning for his loss, the drab hat and wide cloak since worn by the dervishes of his order.

It was about this time, also, that he first instituted the musical services observed by that order, as they perform their peculiar waltzing. All men took to music and dancing in consequence. Fanatics objected, out of envy. They said Jelāl was gone mad, even as the chiefs of Mekka had said of old of the Prophet. His supposed malady was attributed to the malefic influence of Shemsu-'d-Dīn of Tebrīz.

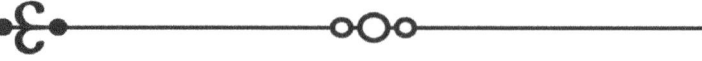

10.

The widow of Jelāl, Kirā (*or* Girā) Khātūn, a model of virtue, the Mary of her age, is related to have seen, through a chink in the door of the room where he and Shems were closeted in spiritual communion, that the wall suddenly opened, and six men of majestic mien entered by the cleft.

These strangers, who were of the occult saints, saluted, bowed, and laid a nosegay at the feet of Jelāl, although it was then in the depth of the midwinter season. They remained until near the hour of dawn worship, when they motioned to Shemsu-'d-Dīn to act as leader on the occasion of the service. He excused himself, and Jelāl performed the office. The service of worship over, the six strangers took leave, and passed out by the same cleft in the wall.

Jelāl now came forth from the chamber, bringing the nosegay in his hand. Seeing his wife in the passage, he gave her the nosegay, saying that the strangers had brought it as an offering to her.

The next day, she sent her servant, with a few leaves from her nosegay, to the perfumers' mart of the city, to inquire what might be the flowers composing it, as she had never seen their like before. The merchants were all equally astonished; no one had ever seen such leaves.

At length, however, a spice merchant from India, who was then sojourning in Qonya, saw those leaves, and knew them to be the petals of a flower that grows in the south of India, in the neighbourhood of Ceylon.

The wonder now was: How did these Indian flowers get to Qonya; and in the depth of winter, too?

The servant carried the leaves back, and reported to his lady what he had learnt. This increased her astonishment a hundredfold. Just then Jelāl made his appearance, and enjoined on her to take the greatest care of the nosegay, as it had been sent to her by the florists of the lost earthly paradise, through those Indian saints, as a special offering.

It is related that she preserved them as long as she lived, merely giving a few leaves, with Jelāl's express permission, to the Georgian wife of the king. If any one suffered with any disease of the eyes, one leaf from that nosegay, applied to the ailing part, was an instant cure. The flowers never lost their fragrance or freshness. What is musk compared with such?

11.

To prove that man lives through God's will alone, and not by blood, Jelāl one day, in the presence of a crowd of physicians and philosophers, had the veins of both his arms opened, and allowed them to bleed until they ceased to flow. He then ordered incisions to be made in various parts of his body; but not one drop of moisture was anywhere obtainable. He now went to a hot bath, washed, performed an ablution, and then commenced the exercise of the sacred dance.

12.

One of Jelāl's disciples died, and there was a consultation among his friends as to whether he should be buried in a coffin or without one.

Another disciple, after Jelāl had been consulted, and had told them to do as they pleased, made the observation that it would be better to bury their relative without a coffin. On being asked why, he answered: "A mother can better nurse her child, than can her child's brother. The earth is the mother of the human race, and the wood of a coffin is also the earth's child; therefore, the coffin is the man's brother. Man's corpse should be committed, then, not to a coffin, but to mother earth, his loving, affectionate parent."

Jelāl expressed his admiration for this apposite and sublime doctrine, which, he said, was not to be found written in any then extant book.

The name of the disciple who made this beautiful remark was Kerīmu-'d-Dīn, son of Begh-Tīmūr.

13.

Many of the chief disciples of Jelāl have related that he himself explained to them, as his reasons for instituting the musical service of his order, with their dancing, the following reflections:—

"God has a great regard for the Roman people. In answer to a prayer of the first Caliph, Abū-Bekr, God made the Romans a chief receptacle of His mercy; and the land of the Romans (Asia

Minor) is the most beautiful on the face of the earth. But the people of the land were utterly void of all idea of the riches of a love towards God, and of the remotest shade of a taste for the delights of the inner, spiritual life. The great Causer of all causes caused a source of affection to arise, and out of the wilderness of causelessness raised a means by which I was attracted away from the land of Khurāsān to the country of the Romans. That country He made a home for my children and posterity, in order that, with the elixir of His grace, the copper of their existences might be transmuted into gold and into philosopher-stone, they themselves being received into the communion of saints. When I perceived that they had no inclination for the practice of religious austerities, and no knowledge of the divine mysteries, I imagined to arrange metrical exhortations and musical services, as being captivating for men's minds, and more especially so for the Romans, who are naturally of a lively disposition, and fond of incisive expositions. Even as a sick child is coaxed into taking a salutary, though nauseous medicine, so, in like manner, were the Romans led by art to acquire a taste for spiritual truth."

14.

As an instance of the great value attached to the poetry of Jelāl, the following anecdote is related:—

Shemsu-'d-Dīn Hindi, Prince of Shiraz in the province of Fars, Southern Persia), wrote a flattering letter to the renowned poet, Sheykh Sa'dī, of Shīrāz (who lived A.H. 571-691, A.D. 1175-1291, and was consequently a contemporary of Jelāl's), begging him to select the best ode, with the most sublime thoughts, that he knew

of as existing in Persian, and to send it to him, for presentation to the great Khān of the Moguls (who then ruled over nearly all Asia).

It so happened that the ode by Jelāl had just become known at Shiraz, which commences:—

"Divine love's voice each instant left and right is heard to sound,
 We're bound for heaven. To witness our departure who'll be found'?"

This ode had captivated the minds of all the men of culture in the city; and this ode Sa'dī selected, wrote it out, and sent it to the prince, with the remark: "A monarch, of auspicious advent, has sprung up in the land of Rome, from whose privacy these are some of the breathings. Never have more beautiful words been uttered, and never will be. Would that I could go to Rome, and rub my face in the dust under his feet!"

The prince thanked Sa'dī exceedingly, and sent him valuable presents in return. Eventually, Sa'dī did go to "Rome," arrived in Qonya, and had the gratification to kiss the hand of Jelāl. He was well received in that city by the dervish circle.

The prince was himself a disciple of Sheykh .... 'd-Dīn, of Bakharz (in Khurāsān, about midway between Tūrshīz and Herāt), to whom he sent a copy of the ode, to learn what the Sheykh would think of it. All the learned men of Bakharz assembled round the Sheykh. He read the ode attentively, and then burst out into exclamations of the wildest delight and most fervid admiration, rending his garments, and acting as though mad. At length he

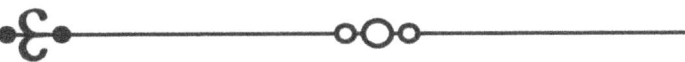

calmed down and said: "O wonderful man! O thou champion of the Faith! Thou pole of the heavens and of the earth! Verily, thou art a wonderful Sultan, who hast appeared on earth! In good sooth, all the Sheykhs of bygone ages who were seers, have been frustrated in not having seen this man! They would have supplicated the Lord of Truth to allow them to meet him! But it was not to be; and this mercy will last until the end of time, as has been sung:—

"A fortune, by the men of ancient times in dreams long sought,
 Has been vouchsafed to modern men; without their efforts caught."

"One ought to put on ironed shoes, and take in hand an ironed staff, to set out at once and visit this great light. I make it a legacy to all my friends to do so without the least delay, if they have the means and the strength, so as to achieve the happiness and secure the honour of making the acquaintance of this prince, so obtaining the grace and favour of hearing him. His father, Bahā Veled, and his ancestors, were great Sheykhs and most illustrious; their great progenitor having been the first Caliph, Abū-Bekr, the glorious Confirmer of the truth spoken by the Apostle of God. I am myself old and infirm, unequal to the fatigues of travel. Otherwise, I would have walked, not on the soles of my feet, but on the tips of my great toes, to visit that eminent man."

The Sheykh's eldest son, Muzahhiru-'d-Dīn, was there present. To him the Sheykh addressed himself, saying: "My son, I do hope that thy eyes will behold this sacred visage; and, if God so will, convey to him my salutation and my respects."

After the death of the old man, his son went to Rome, had the felicity to see Jelāl, and presented his father's message. He returned to Bakharz; but it is said that a son of his lies buried at Qonya.

15.

Kirā Khātūn, the widow of Jelāl, is reported to have related to a friend that there was in their household a candlestick of the height of a man, before which Jelāl used to stand on foot the night through, until daydawn, studying the writings of his father.

One night, a company of the genii, dwellers in the college where Jelāl and his wife lived, appeared to her in a body, to complain of the great inconvenience and suffering to which they were subjected by this practice of Jelāl's, and saying: "We can put up with it no longer. Take care, lest we do a mischief to some one in the college."

The lady reported this complaint of the genii to her husband. He merely smiled, and took no further notice of the matter for several days.

At the end of that time, however, he spoke of it, and told his wife to trouble herself no more about the threat of the genii, as he had converted them all. They had become disciples of his, and would certainly do no harm to any friend or dependent of their teacher.

16.

It was related by one of the chief of Jelāl's disciples, a butcher by trade, a trainer of dogs for the chase, and a purveyor of horses of

the best kind, which he used to sell to princes and grandees at high prices, that, at a certain time, Jelāl was much exercised by visions from the spiritual world, so that for forty days he was as though beside himself, passing through the streets with his head bare, and his turban twisted round his neck.

After that, he came suddenly one day, bathed in perspiration, to the butcher, and said he wanted a certain unbroken horse to be saddled for him immediately. The butcher, with the help of three stable-men, managed with the utmost difficulty to saddle the horse and bring him out. Jelāl mounted him without opposition, and set off in a southerly direction. The butcher asked whether he should accompany him, and Jelāl replied: "Give me your prayers and holy good wishes."

In the evening Jelāl returned covered with dust. The poor horse, though of gigantic frame, was reduced to mere skin and bone, being nearly broken-backed with fatigue.

The next day he came again, and asked for another horse, better than the one of yesterday, mounted it, and rode off. He returned at the hour of sunset devotions, and this horse also was reduced to a pitiable condition. The butcher dared not offer a word of remonstrance.

On the third day he came again, mounted a third horse, and returned as before, at sunset. He sat down now in the most composed manner possible, and called out cheerily: "Good news! Glad tidings, O ye of the Faith! That dog of hell has gone back to his pit of fire!"

The butcher was too much astonished at his manner to feel any inclination to inquire what these words might mean; but a certain number of days afterwards, a large caravan came into Qonya from Syria, and brought news that the Mogul army had besieged Damascus, and had reduced it to straits.

Helaw Khan (Holagu, Helagu) had taken Bagdad in A.H. 655 (A.D. 1257-58). Two years later, A.H. 657 (A.D. 1259-60), he advanced against Aleppo and Syria, sending his general, Ketbuga, against Damascus with a numerous army. He laid siege to the city. But the inhabitants witnessed, with their very own eyes, that Jelāl came and joined himself there to the forces of Islām. He inflicted defeat on the Mogul forces, who were compelled to retreat, totally frustrated.

The butcher was overjoyed at this welcome intelligence, and went forthwith to communicate the news to Jelāl. The latter smilingly replied: "Yes, yes! Jelālu-'d-Dīn was the horseman who obtained a victory over the enemy, and showed himself a Sultan in the eyes of the people of Islām." On hearing this, his disciples rent the air with their shouts of joy and triumph, and the townspeople of Qonya decked out and illuminated the city, holding public rejoicings.

This miracle of power became noised abroad, and everywhere Jelāl's friends and adherents were transported with ecstasy at its occurrence.

17.

On one occasion a rich merchant of Tebrīz came to Qonya. He inquired of his agents there who was the most eminent man of learning and piety in the city, as he wished to go and pay his respects to him. He remarked to them: "It is not merely for the sake of making money that I travel about in every country on earth; I desire also to make the acquaintance of every man of eminence I can find in each city."

His correspondents told him that the Sheykhu-'l-Islām of the capital had a great reputation for learning and piety, and that they would be proud to present him to that celebrated luminary. Accordingly, he selected a number of rarities from among his store, to the value of thirty sequins; and the party set out to visit the great lawyer.

The merchant found the dignitary lodged in a great palace, with guards at the gate, crowds of servants and attendants in the courtyard, and eunuchs, pages, grooms, ushers, chamberlains, and the like, in the halls.

Turning to his conductors, he expressed some doubt as to whether they had not, by mistake, brought him to the king's palace. They quieted his fears, and led him into the presence of the great fountain of legal erudition. He felt a very great dislike for all he saw; and he remarked to his friends: "A great lawyer is never anything the worse for possessing a clear conscience. A physician may himself indulge in sweetmeats; but he does not prescribe them to a patient suffering with fever."

He now offered his presents; and then inquired of the great lawyer whether he could solve a doubt under which he was then labouring. This he stated as follows:—"Of late, I have been sustaining a series of losses. Can you indicate a way by which I may escape from that unfortunate position? I give, every year, the fortieth part of my liable possessions to the poor; and I distribute alms besides, to the extent of my power. I cannot conceive, therefore, why I am unfortunate."

Other remarks he made also to the same effect. They appeared to be lost on the great luminary, who affected to be otherwise preoccupied. At length the merchant took leave without obtaining a solution to his difficulty.

The day following he inquired of his friends whether there did not chance to be, in the great city, some poor mendicant of exemplary piety, to whom he might offer his respects, and from whom he might, haply, learn what he longed to know, together with advice that would be of service to him. They answered: "Just such a man as thou describest is our Lord, Jelálu-'d-Dín. He has forsaken all pleasures, save only his love towards God. Not only has he given up all concern for worldly matters, he has also renounced all care as to a future state. He passes his nights, as well as his days, in the worship of God; and he is a very ocean of knowledge in all temporal and spiritual subjects."

The Tebríz merchant was enchanted with this information. He begged to see that holy man, the bare mention of whose virtues had filled him with delight. They accordingly conducted him to the college of Jelál, the merchant having privately furnished

himself with a rouleau of fifty sequins in gold as his offering to the saint.

When they reached the college, Jelāl was sitting alone in the lecture-hall, immersed in the study of some books. The party made their obeisances, and the merchant felt himself completely overpowered at the aspect of the venerable teacher; so that he burst .into tears, and could not utter a word. Jelāl addressed him, therefore, as follows:—

"The fifty sequins thou hast provided as thy offering are accepted. But better for thee than these are the two hundred sequins thou hast lost. God, whose glory be exalted, had determined to visit thee with a sore judgment and a heavy trial; but, through this thy visit here, He hath pardoned thee, and the trial is averted from thee. Be not dismayed. From this day forth thou shalt not suffer loss; and that which thou hast already suffered shall be made up to thee."

The merchant was equally astonished and delighted at these words; more so, however, when Jelāl proceeded with his discourse: "The cause and reason of thy bygone losses and misfortunes was, that, on a certain day thou wast in the west of Firengistān (Europe), where thou wentest into a certain ward of a certain city, and there sawest a poor Firengī (European) man, one of the greatest of God's cherished saints, who was lying stretched out at the corner of a market-place. As thou didst pass by him, thou spattest on him, evincing aversion from him. His heart was grieved by thy act and demeanour. Hence the visitations that have

afflicted thee. Go thou, then, and make thy peace with him, asking his forgiveness, and offering him our salutations."

The merchant was petrified at this announcement. Jelāl then asked him: "Wilt thou that we this instant show him to thee?" So saying, he placed his hand on the wall of the apartment, and told the merchant to behold. Instantly, a doorway opened in the wall, and the merchant thence perceived that man in Firengistān, lying down in a market-place. At this sight he bowed down his head and rent his garments, coming away from the saintly presence in a state of stupor. He remembered all these incidents as facts.

Immediately commencing his preparations, he set out without delay, and reached the city in question. He inquired for the ward he wished to visit, and for the man whom he had offended. Him he discovered lying down, stretched out as Jelāl had shown him. The merchant dismounted from his beast, and made his obeisance to the prostrate Firengī dervish, who at once addressed him thus: "What wilt thou that I do? Our Lord Jelāl suffereth me not; or otherwise, I had a desire to make thee see the power of God, and what I am. But now, draw near."

The Firengī dervish then clasped the merchant to his bosom, kissed him repeatedly on both cheeks, and then added: "Look now, that thou mayest see my Lord and Teacher, my spiritual Master, and that thou mayest witness a marvel." The merchant looked. He saw the Lord Jelāl immersed in a holy dance, chanting this hymn, and entranced with sacred music:—

"His kingdom's vast and pure; each sort its fitting place finds there;

Cornelian, ruby, clod, or pebble be thou on His hill.
Believe, He seeks thee; disbelieve, He'll haply cleanse thee fair;
Be here a faithful Abū-Bekr; Firengī there; at will."

When the merchant happily reached Qonya on his return, he gave the salutations of the Firengī saint, and his respects, to Jelāl; and distributed much substance among the disciples. He settled at Qonya, and became a member of the fraternity of the Pure Lovers of God.

18.

Jelāl was one day passing by a street, where two men were quarrelling. He stood on one side. One of the men called out to the other: "Say what thou will; thou shalt hear from me a thousandfold for every word thou mayest utter."

Hereupon Jelāl stepped forward and addressed this speaker, saying: "No, no! Whatsoever thou have to say, say it to me; and for every thousand thou mayest say to me, thou shalt hear from me one word."

On hearing this rebuke, the adversaries were abashed, and made their peace with one another.

19.

One day, a very learned professor brought all his pupils to pay their respects to Jelāl.

On their way to him, the young men agreed together to put some questions to Jelāl on certain points of Arabic grammar, with the

design of comparing his knowledge in that science with that of their professor, whom they looked upon as unequalled.

When they were seated, Jelāl addressed them on various fitting subjects for a while, and thereby paved the way for the following anecdote

"An ingenuous jurist was once travelling with an Arabic grammarian, and they chanced to come to a ruinous well.

The jurist hereupon began to recite the text (of Qur'ān xxii. 44): And of a ruined well.'

"The Arabic word for 'well' he pronounced 'bīr,' with the vowel long. To this the grammarian instantly objected, telling the jurist to pronounce that word with a short vowel and hiatus—bi'r, so as to be in accord with the requirements of classical purity.

"A dispute now arose between the two on the point. It lasted all the rest of the day, and well on into a pitchy dark night; every author being ransacked by them, page by page, each sustaining his own theory of the word. No conclusion was arrived at, and each disputant remained of his own opinion still.

"It so happened in the dark, that the grammarian slipped into the well, and fell to the bottom. There he set up a wail of entreaty: 'O my most courteous fellow-traveller, lend thy help to extricate me from this most darksome pit.'

"The jurist at once expressed his most pleasurable willingness to lend him that help, with only one trifling condition—that he should confess himself in error, and consent to suppress the hiatus in the word 'bi'r.' The grammarian's answer was 'Never.' So in the well he remained."

"Now," said Jelāl, "to apply this to yourselves. Unless you will consent to cast out from your hearts the '*hiatus*' of indecision and of self-love, you can never hope to escape from the noisome pit of self-worship,—the well of man's nature and of fleshly lusts. The dungeon of Joseph's well' in the human breast is this very 'self-worship;' and from it you will not escape, nor will you ever attain to those heavenly regions—'the spacious land of God'" (Qur'ān iv. 99, xxix. 56, xxxix. 13).

On hearing these pregnant words, the whole assembly of undergraduates uncovered their heads, and with fervent zeal professed themselves his spiritual disciples.

20.

There was a great and good governor (apparently) of Qonya, of the name of Mu'īnu-'d-Dīn, whose title was the Perwāna (moth or fly-wheel, viz., of the far-distant Mogul Emperor, resident at the court of the king). He was a great friend to the dervishes, to the learned, and to Jelāl, whose loving disciple he was.

One day, a company of the dervishes and learned men united in extolling the Perwāna to the skies, in Jelāl's presence. He assented to all they advanced in that respect, and added: "The Perwāna merits a hundredfold all your eulogiums. But there is another side to the question, which may be exemplified by the following anecdote:—

"A company of pilgrims were once proceeding towards Mekka, when the camel of one of the party fell down in the desert, totally exhausted. The camel could not be got to rise again. Its load was, therefore, transferred to another beast, the fallen brute was abandoned to its fate, and the caravan resumed its journey.

"Ere long the fallen camel was surrounded by a circle of ravenous wild beasts,—wolves, jackals, etc. But none of these ventured to attack hint. The members of the caravan became aware of this singularity, and one of them went back to investigate the matter. He found that an amulet had been left suspended on the animal's neck; and this he removed. When he had retreated to a short distance, the hungry brutes fell upon the poor camel, and soon tore him piecemeal."

"Now," said Jelāl, "this world is in an exactly similar category with that poor camel. The learned of the world are the company of pilgrims, and our (Jelāl's) existence among them is the amulet suspended round the neck of the camel—the world. So long as we remain so suspended, the world will go on, the caravan will proceed. But so soon as the divine mandate shall be spoken: 'O thou submissive spirit, come thou back to thy Lord, content and approved' (Qur'ān lxxxix. 2 7-8), and we be removed from the neck of the world-camel, people will see how it shall fare with the world, how its inhabitants shall be driven,—what shall become of its sultans, its doctors, its scribes."

It is said that these words were spoken a short time before Jelāl's death. When he departed this life, not much time elapsed ere the Sultan, with many of his great men of learning and nobles,

followed him to the grave, while troubles of all kinds overwhelmed the land for a season, until God again vouchsafed it peace.

21.

During one of his expositions, Jelāl said: "Thou seest naught, save that thou seest God therein."

A dervish came forward and raised the objection that the term "therein" indicated a receptacle, whereas it could not be predicated of God that He is comprehensible by any receptacle, as this would imply a contradiction in terms. Jelāl answered him as follows:—

"Had not that unimpeachable proposition been true, we had not proffered it. There is therein, forsooth, a contradiction in terms; but it is a contradiction in time, so that the receptacle and the recepted may differ,—may be two distinct things; even as the universe of God's qualities is the receptacle of the universe of God's essence. But, these two universes are really one. The first of them is not He; the second of them is not other than He. Those, apparently, two things are in truth one and the same. How, then, is a contradiction in terms implied? God comprises the exterior and the interior. If we cannot say He is the interior, He will not include the interior. But He comprises all, and in Him all things have their being. He is, then, the receptacle also, comprising all existences, as the Qur'ān (xli. 54) says: 'He comprises all things.'"

The dervish was convinced, bowed, and declared himself a disciple.

22.

Jelāl was one day seated in the shop of his great disciple the Goldbeater, Salāhu-'d-Dīn; and was surrounded by a circle of other disciples, listening to his discourse; when an old man came rushing in, beating his breast, and uttering loud lamentations. He entreated Jelāl to help him in his endeavours to recover his little son, a child seven years old, lost for several days past, in spite of every effort made to find him.

Jelāl expressed his disapprobation at the extreme importance the old man appeared to attach to his loss; and said: "Mankind in general have lost their God. Still, one does not hear that they go about in quest of Him, beating their breasts and making a great noise. What, then, has happened to thee so very particular, that thou makest all this fuss, and degradest thyself, an elder, by these symptoms of grief for the loss of a little child? Why seekest thou not for a time the Lord of the whole world, begging assistance of Him, that peradventure thy lost Joseph may be found, and thou be comforted, as was Jacob on the recovery of his child?"

The old man at once followed Jelāl's advice, and begged forgiveness of God. Just then, news was brought him there that his son had been found. Many who were witnesses of these circumstances became devoted followers of Jelāl.

23.

Jelāl was one day lecturing, when a young man of distinction came in, pushed his way, and took a seat higher up than an old man, one of the audience.

Jelāl at once remarked: "In days of yore it was the command of God, that, if any young man should take precedence of an elder, the earth should at once swallow him up; such being the divine punishment for that offence. Now, however, I see that young men, barely out of leading-strings, show no respect for age, but trample over those in years. They have no dread of the earth's swallowing them up, nor any fear of being transformed into apes. (4) It happened, however, that one morning the Victorious Lion of God, 'Alī, son of Abū-Tālib, was hasting from his house to perform his devotions at dawn in the mosque of the Prophet. On his way, he overtook an old man, a Jew, who was going in the same direction. The future Caliph, out of innate nobility and politeness of nature, had respect for the Jew's age, and would not pass him, though the Jew's pace was slow. When 'Alī reached the mosque, the Prophet was already bowed down in his devotions; and was about to chant the *'Gloria,'* but, by God's command, Gabriel came down, laid his hand on the Prophet's shoulder, and stopped him, lest 'Alī should lose the merit attaching to his being present at the opening of the dawn service; for it is more meritorious to perform that early service once, than to fulfil the devotions of a hundred years at other hours of the day. The Prophet has said: 'The first act of reverence at dawn worship is of more value than the world and all that is therein.'

"When the Apostle of God had concluded his *worship*, offered up his *customary prayers*, and recited his usual *lessons* from the Qur'ān, he turned, and asked of Gabriel the occult cause of his interruption at that time. Gabriel replied that God had not seen fit that 'Alī should be deprived of the merit attaching to the performance of the first portion of the dawn worship, through the respect he had shown to the old Jew he had overtaken, but whom he would not pass.

"Now," remarked Jelāl, "when a saint like 'Alī showed so much respect for a poor old misbelieving Jew, and when God viewed his respectful consideration in so highly favourable a manner, you may all infer how He will view any honour and veneration shown to an elderly saint of approved piety, whose beard has grown grey in the service of God, and whose companions are the elect of their Maker, whose chosen servant he is; and what reward He will mete out in consequence. For, in truth, glory and power belong to God, to the Apostle, and to the believers, as God hath Himself declared (Qur'ān lxiii. 8): 'Unto God belongeth the power, and to the apostle, and to the believers.'

"If then," added he, "ye wish to be prosperous in your affairs, take fast hold on the skirts of your spiritual elders. For, without the blessing of his pious elders, a young man will never live to be old, and will never attain the station of a spiritual elder."

24.

One day Jelāl took as his text the following words (Qur'ān xxxi. 18):—"Verily, the most discordant of all sounds is the voice of the asses." He then put the question: "Do my friends know what this signifies?"

The congregation all bowed, and entreated him to expound it to them. Jelāl therefore proceeded:—

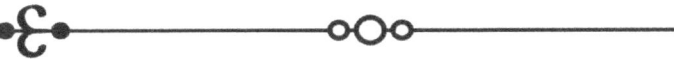

"All other brutes have a *cry*, a *lesson*, and a *doxology*, with which they commemorate their Maker and Provider. Such are, the *yearning cry* of the camel, the *roar* of the lion, the *bleat* of the gazelle, the *buzz* of the fly, the *hum*, of the bee, etc.

"The angels in heaven, and the genii, have their doxologies also, even as man has his doxology—his *Magnificat*, and various forms of worship for his heart (or mind) and for his body.

"The poor ass, however, has nothing but his *bray*. He sounds this bray on two occasions only: when he desires his female, and when he feels hunger. He is the slave of his lust and of his gullet.

"In like manner, if man have not in his heart a doxology for God, a cry, and a love, together with a secret and a care in his mind, he is less than an ass in God's esteem; for He has said (Qur'ān vii. 178): 'They are like the camels; nay, they are yet more erring.'" He then related the following anecdote:—

"In bygone days there was a monarch, who, by way of trial, requested another sovereign to send him three things, the worst of their several kinds that he could procure; namely, the worst article of food, the worst dispositioned thing, and the worst animal.

"The sovereign so applied to sent him some cheese, as the worst food; an Armenian slave, as the worst-dispositioned thing; and an ass, as the worst of animals. In the superscription to the epistle sent with these offerings, the sovereign quoted the verse of Scripture pointed out above."

25.

On a certain day, the Lord Jelālu-'d-Dīn went forth to the country residence of the saint Husāmu-'d-Dīn, riding on an ass. He remarked: "This is the saddle-beast of the righteous. Several of the prophets have ridden on asses: as Seth, Ezra, Jesus, and Muhammed."

It so chanced that one of his disciples was also mounted on an ass. The creature suddenly began to bray; and the rider, annoyed at the occurrence, struck the ass on the head several times.

Jelāl remonstrated: "Why strike the poor brute? Strikest thou him because he bears thy burden? Returnest thou not thanks for that thou art the rider, and he the vehicle? Suppose now, which God forbid, that the reverse were the case. What wouldst thou have done? His cry arises from one or the other of two causes, his gullet or his lust. In this respect, he shares the common lot of all creatures. They are all continually thus actuated. All, then, would have to be scolded and beaten over the head."

The disciple was abashed. He dismounted, kissed the hoof of his ass, and caressed him.

26.

On a certain occasion, one of his disciples complained to Jelāl of the scantiness of his means and the extent of his needs. Jelāl answered: "Out upon thee! Get thee gone! Henceforward, count me not a friend of thine; and so, peradventure, wealth may come to thee." He then related the following anecdote:—

"It happened, once, that a certain disciple of the Prophet said to him: 'I love thee!' The Prophet answered: 'Why tarriest thou, then? Haste to put on a breastplate of steel, and set thy face to encounter misfortunes. Prepare thyself, also, to endure straitness, the special gift of the friends and lovers (of God and His Apostle)!'"

Another anecdote, also, he thus narrated: "A Gnostic adept once asked of a rich man which he loved best, riches or sin. The latter answered that he loved riches best. The other replied: 'Thou sayest not the truth. Thou better lovest sin and calamity. Seest thou not that thou leavest thy riches behind, whilst thou carriest thy sin and thy calamity about with thee, making thyself reprehensible in the sight of God! Be a man! Exert thyself to carry thy riches with thee, and sin not; since thou lovest thy riches. What thou hast to do is this: Send thy riches to God ere thou goest before Him thyself; peradventure, they may work thee some advantage; even as God hath said (Qur'ān lxxiii. 20): 'And that which ye send before, for your souls, of good works, shall ye find with God. He is the best and the greatest in rewarding.'"

27.

It is related that one day the Perwāna, Mu'īnu-'d-Dīn, held a great assembly in his palace. To this meeting were collected together all the Doctors of the Law, the Sheykhs, the men of piety, the recluses, and the strangers who had congregated from various lands.

The chiefs of the law had taken their places in the highest seats. The Perwāna had had a great desire that Jelāl should honour the

assembly with his presence. He had a son-in-law, Mejdu-'d-Dín, governor to the young princes, the sons of the king. This son-in-law of his was a disciple of Jelāl's, and a man of very eminent qualities, with great faith in his teacher. He offered to go and invite Jelāl to the meeting.

Hereupon, the arch-sower of doubts and animosities in the human breast spread among the chiefs of the law, there present, the suspicion that, if Jelāl should come, the question of precedence would arise: "Where should he be seated?" They all agreed that they were themselves in their proper places, and that Jelāl must find a seat where he could.

Mejdu-'d-Dín delivered the Perwāna's courteous message to his teacher. Jelāl, inviting Husāmu-'d-Dín and others of his disciples to accompany him, set out for the Perwāna's palace. The disciples went on a little ahead, and Jelāl brought up the procession.

When Husām entered the apartment of the Perwāna, all present rose to receive him, making room for him in the upper seats. Lastly, Jelāl made his appearance.

The Perwāna and other courtiers crowded forward to receive Jelāl with honour, and kissed His Lordship's blessed hands with reverence, expressing regret that he had been put to inconvenience by his condescension. He returned compliment for compliment, and was shown upstairs.

On reaching the assembly room, he saw that the grandees had occupied the whole of the sofa, from end to end. He saluted them, and prayed for God's grace to be showered upon them;

seating himself then in the middle of the floor. Husāmu-'d-Dīn immediately rose from his seat, descended from the sofa, and took a place by the side of Jelāl.

The grandees of the assembly now arose also, excepting those who, in spite and pride, had formed the confederacy mentioned above. These kept their seats. Some of them were of the greatest eminence in learning; and one, especially, was not only very learned, but also eloquent, witty, and bold?

He, seeing what had taken place, and that all the men of rank had quitted the sofa, to seat themselves on the floor, asked in a jocose manner: "Where, according to the rules of the Order, is the chief seat in an assembly?"

Some one answered him: "In an assembly of the learned, the chief seat is in the middle of the sofa, where the professor always sits." Another added: "With recluses, the cell of solitude is the chief seat." A third said: "In the convents of dervish brethren, the chief seat is the lower end of the sofa, where, in reality, people put off their shoes."

After these remarks, some one present, as an experiment, asked Jelāl, saying: "In your rule and opinion, where is the chief seat?" His answer was: "The chief seat is that where one's beloved is found." The interrogator now asked: "And where is your beloved?" Jelāl replied: "Thou must be blind, not to see."

Jelāl then arose, and began to sing. Many joined; and the singing became so enthusiastic, that the nobles rent their garments.

It so happened that, after Jelāl's death, this interlocutor of his went to Damascus, and there became blind. Friends flocked to visit him, and to condole with him. He wept bitterly, and cried aloud: "Alas, alas! what have I not suffered? That very moment, when Jelāl gave me that fatal answer, a black veil seemed to fall down over my eyes, so that I could not distinguish objects clearly, or their colours. But I have hope and faith in him, that, out of his sublime generosity, he will yet take pity on me, and pardon my presumption. The goodness of the saints is infinite; and Jelāl himself hath said: 'Despair not because of one sin; for the ocean of divine mercy accepteth penitence.'"

The foregoing incident is also related with the following variation:—

Shemsu-'d-Dīn of Tebrīz had just then returned to Qonya, and was among those who accompanied Jelāl to the Perwāna's palace, sitting down near him on the floor. When the question was put: "Where is your beloved?" Jelāl arose, and cast himself on the breast of Shems. That occurrence it was that made Shems, from that time forward, a man of mark in all Qonya.

28.

There was in Qonya a great physician, of eminence and ability, who used occasionally to visit Jelāl.

On one of those days, Jelāl requested him to prepare seventeen purgative draughts by a certain time, propitious for taking medicine, as that number of his friends required them.

When the specified time came, Jelāl went to the physician's house, and received the seventeen draughts. He immediately began, and, in the physician's presence, drank off the whole seventeen in succession, thence returning home.

The physician followed him there, to render the assistance he felt sure would be wanted. He found Jelāl seated as usual, in perfect health, and lecturing to his disciples. On inquiring how he felt, Jelāl answered, in the words so often repeated in the Qur'ān (ii. 23, etc.): "Beneath which rivers flow." The physician recommended Jelāl to abstain from water. Jelāl instantly ordered ice to be brought and broken up small. Of this he swallowed an inordinate quantity, while the physician looked on.

Jelāl then went to a hot-bath. After bathing, he began to sing and dance; continuing in those exercises three whole days and nights, without intermission.

The physician declared this to be the greatest miracle ever wrought by prophet or by saint. With his whole family, and with many of the greatest in the medical profession, he joined himself to the multitude of Jelāl's disciples of the most sincere.

29.

The Perwāna is related to have said publicly, in his own palace, that Jelāl was a matchless monarch, no sovereign having ever appeared in any age like unto him; but that his disciples were a very disreputable set.

These words were reported to them, and the company of disciples were greatly scandalised at the imputation. Jelāl sent a note to the Perwāna, of which the following is the substance:—

"Had my disciples been good men, I had been their disciple. Inasmuch as they were bad, I accepted them as my disciples, that they might reform and become good - of the company of the righteous. By the soul of my father, they were not accepted as disciples, until God had made Himself responsible that they would attain to mercy and grace, admitted among those accepted of Him. Until that assurance was given, they were not received by me, nor had they any place in the hearts of the servants of God. 'The sons of grace are saved; the children of wrath are sick; for the sake of Thy mercy, we, a people of wrath, have come to Thee.'"

When the Perwāna had read and considered these words, he became still more attached to Jelāl; arose, came to him, asked pardon, and prayed for forgiveness of God, distributing largely of his bounty among the disciples.

30.

Another great and good man once observed: "Jelāl is a great saint and a sovereign; but he must be dragged forth from among his disciples." This was reported to Jelāl, who smiled, and said: "If he can!"

Soon afterwards he added: "Why, then, is it that my followers are looked upon with spite by the men of the world? It is because they are beloved of God, and favourably regarded by Him. I have sifted all mankind; and all have fallen through my sieve, excepting these friends of mine. They have remained. My existence is the life of my friends, and the existence of my friends is the life of the men of the world, whether they know this, or whether they ignore it."

31.

There was a young merchant, whose house was near Jelāl's college, and who had professed himself a sincere and ardent disciple.

He conceived a desire and intention to make a voyage to Egypt; but his friends tried to dissuade him. His intention was reported to Jelāl, who strictly and rigorously prohibited his undertaking the voyage.

The young man could not divest himself of his desire, and had no peace of mind; so one night he clandestinely stole away, and went off to Syria. Arrived at Antioch, he embarked in a ship, and set sail. As God had willed, his ship was taken by Firengī pirates. He was made prisoner, and was confined in a deep dungeon, where he had a daily portion of food doled out to him, barely sufficient to keep his body and soul together.

He was thus kept imprisoned forty days, during which he wept bitterly, and reproached himself for having been disobedient to the injunction of Jelāl; saying: "This is the reward of my crime. I have disobeyed the command of my sovereign, following after my own evil propensity."

Precisely on the night of the fortieth day, he saw Jelāl in a dream, who addressed him, and said: "To-morrow, to whatever questions these misbelievers may ask thee, do thou return the answer: 'I know.' By that means shalt, thou be released." He awoke bewildered, returned thanks to Heaven, and sat down in holy meditation, awaiting the solution of the dream.

Shortly, he saw a company of Firengī people come to him, with whom was an interpreter. They asked him: "Knowest thou aught of philosophy, and canst thou practise therapeutics? Our prince is sick." His answer was: "I know."

They immediately took him out of the pit, led him to a bath, and dressed him in a handsome vestment of honour. They then conducted him to the residence of the sick man.

The young merchant, inspired of God, ordered them to bring him seven fruits. These he prepared with a little scammony, and made the whole into a draught, which he administered to the patient.

By the grace of God, and the intercession of the saints, his treatment was crowned with success, after two or three visits. The Firengī prince recovered; and by reason that the favour of Jelāl was upon that young merchant, though he was utterly illiterate, he became a philosopher. Jelāl assisted him.

When the Firengī prince had entirely recovered his health, and had arisen from his sick-bed, he told the young merchant to ask of him whatsoever he might wish. He asked for his freedom, and for leave to return home, that he might rejoin his teacher. He then related all that had befallen him;—his disobedience, his vision,

and the assistance of Jelāl. The whole audience of Firengīs, without sight of Jelāl, became believers in him, and wooers of him.

They set the young merchant free, and allowed him to depart, bestowing on him rich presents and a bountiful outfit.

On his arrival at the metropolis, before going to his own house, he hastened to pay his respects to Jelāl. On beholding the sacred features from afar, he threw himself on the earth, embraced Jelāl's two feet, kissed them, rubbed his face upon them, and wept. Jelāl raised him, kissed both his cheeks, and said: "It was a narrow escape through thy curing the Firengī prince. Thou didst abscond; but henceforward, do thou remain at home, and occupy thyself in earning what is lawful. Take contentment as thy exemplar. The sufferings of the sea, the commotion of the ship, the calamity of captivity, and the darkness of the dungeon, are so many evils. Contentment is a very blessing from God."

32.

Jelāl one day was going from his college into the town, when by chance he met a Christian monk, who made him an obeisance. Jelāl asked him which was the elder, himself or his beard. The monk replied: "I am twenty years older than my beard. It came forth that number of years later." Jelāl answered him "Then I pity thee. Thy young beard has attained to maturity, whereas thou hast remained immature, as thou wast. Thou art as black, and as weak, and as untutored as ever. Alas for thee, if thou change not, and ripen not!"

The poor monk at once renounced his rope girdle, threw it away, professed the faith of Islām, and became a believer.

33.

A company of black-habited ones (Christian priests or monks) chanced to meet Jelāl one day, as they came from a distant place. When his disciples espied them afar off, they expressed their aversion from them by exclaiming: "O the dark-looking, disagreeable things!"

Jelāl remarked: "In the whole world, none are more generous than they are. They have given over to us, in this life, the faith of Islām, purity, cleanliness, and the various modes of worshipping God; while, in the world to come, they have left to us the everlasting abodes of paradise, the large-eyed damsels, and the pavilions, as well as the sight of God, of which they will enjoy no share; for God hath said (Qur'ān vii. 48): 'Verily God hath made both of them forbidden things to the misbelievers!' They walk in darkness and misbelief, willingly incurring the torments of hell. But, let only the sun of righteousness rise upon them suddenly, and they will become believers."

Being now come near enough, they all made their obeisances to Jelāl, entered into conversation with him, and professed themselves true Muslims. Jelāl now turned to his disciples, and added: "God swallows up the darkness in the light, and the light in the darkness. He also makes in the darkness a place for the light." The disciples bowed, and rejoiced.

34.

A certain well-known disciple related that, on one occasion, Jelāl and his friends went forth to the country-seat of Husām, and there held a grand festival of holy music and dancing until near daybreak. Jelāl then left off, to give his followers a little rest.

They dispersed about the grounds; and the narrator took a seat in a spot from whence he could see and observe Jelāl. The others all fell asleep; but he occupied himself with reflections on the miracles performed by various of the prophets and of the saints. He thought to himself: "I wonder whether this holy man works miracles. Of course he does; only, he keeps the fact quiet, to avoid the inconveniences of notoriety."

Hardly had the thought crossed his mind, when Jelāl called him by name. On his approaching Jelāl, the latter stooped, picked up a pebble from the earth, placed it on the back of his own hand, and said to him: "Here, take this; it is thy portion; and be thou one of the thankful" (Qur'ān vii. 141).

The disciple examined the pebble by the light of the moon, and saw that it was a large ruby, exceedingly clear and brilliant, not to be found in the treasuries of kings.

Utterly astounded, he shrieked out, and swooned away; awaking the whole company with his shout; for he was a very loud-voiced man. On recovery, he told the others what had occurred. He also expressed to Jelāl his contrition for the temerity of his reflections.

Jelāl told him to carry the stone to the queen, and to mention how he had become possessed of it. The queen accepted it, had it valued, and gave to him a hundred and eighty thousand pieces of silver in return, besides rich gifts. She also distributed presents to all the members of the fraternity.

35.

A certain sheykh, son of a sheykh, and a man of great reputation for learning, came to Qonya, and was respect- fully visited by all the people of eminence residing there.

It so happened that Jelāl and his friends were gone that day to a mosque in the country; and the new-comer, offended at Jelāl's not basting to visit him, made the remark in public: "Has Jelāl never heard the adage: 'The newly-arrived one is visited'?"

One of Jelāl's disciples chanced to be present, and heard this remark. On the other hand, Jelāl was expounding sublime truths in the mosque to his disciples, when suddenly he exclaimed, "My dear brother! I am the newly-arrived one, not thou. Thou and those like thee are bound to visit me, and so gain honour to yourselves."

All his audience were surprised at this apostrophe; wondering to whom it was addressed. Jelāl then spake a parable: "One man came from Bagdād, and another went forth out of his house and ward; which of the two ought to pay the first visit to the other?"

All agreed in opinion that the man from Bagdād ought to be visited by the other. Then Jelāl explained, thus: "In reality, I am

returned from the Bagdād of *nulliquity*, whereas this dearly beloved son of a sheykh, who has come here, has gone forth from a ward of this world. I am better entitled, therefore, to be visited than is he. I have been hymning in the Bagdād of the world of spirits the heavenly canticle: 'I am the Truth,' since a time anterior to the commencement of the present war, ere the truth obtained its victory." The disciples expressed their concurrence, and rejoiced exceedingly.

By and by, the sheykh's son was informed of this wonder. He at once arose, went on foot to visit Jelāl, uncovered his head, and owned that Jelāl was right. He further declared himself Jelāl's disciple, and said: "My father enjoined me to put on ironed sandals, taking an iron-shod staff in my hand, and go forth in quest of Jelālu-'d-Dīn, since it is a duty of all to visit and reverence him who has spoken the truth and reposes on the truth. But the majesty of Jelāl is a hundredfold greater than what my father explained to me."

36.

Jelāl once commanded one of his attendants to go and arrange a certain matter. The attendant answered: "God willing."

Upon this, Jelāl was wroth, and shouted to him: "Stupid, garrulous fool!" The attendant fainted and foamed at the mouth.

The disciples interceded. Jelāl expressed his forgiveness; and the attendant recovered.

37.

On the occasion of a grand religious commemoration at the house of the Perwāna, in the presence of the Sultan Ruknu-'d-Dīn, this monarch was taken unwell, and the exercises were suspended, only, one of the disciples continued to sing and shout.

The Sultan remarked: "How ill-behaved is that man! Does he pretend to be more ecstatic than his teacher Jelālu-'d-Dīn?"

Jelāl heard this, and answered the king: "Thou art unable to withstand an attack of fever. How then canst thou expect a man devoured with an enthusiasm that threatens to swallow up even heaven itself, to calm down on a sudden?"

When the disciples heard this, they set up a shout; and the Sultan, after himself witnessing one or two of the mighty signs wrought by Jelāl, made his obeisance to him, and became a disciple.

38.

It has been related by some that the final overthrow of the rule of the Seljūqī dynasty in Asia Minor (in A.H. 700, A.D. 1300, was in this manner:—

The Sultan Ruknu-'d-Dīn had adopted Jelāl as his (spiritual) father. After a while, he held a great dervish festival in the palace. But, about that period, a certain Sheykh Bāba had created for himself a great name in Qonya, and certain intriguers had led the king to visit him.

It was shortly after that visit that the king held the revival in honour of Bāba in the Hall of the Bowls.

The sheykh was met and introduced in state by the court officials, and was then installed on the throne, with the Sultan seated on a chair by his side. Jelāl now made his appearance, saluted, and took his seat in a corner of the hall. Portions of the Qur'ān were recited, and exhortations were delivered, with hymns.

The Sultan then turned to Jelāl, and spoke: "Be it known to the Lord Jelāl, to the Doctors of the Law, and to the grandees, that I have adopted the Sheykh Bāba as my, (spiritual) father, who has accepted me as his dutiful and affectionate son."

All present shouted their approval, and prayed for a blessing on the arrangement. But Jelāl, burning with divine jealousy, instantly exclaimed (in words traditionally related of the prophet, Muhammed): "Verily, Sa'd is a jealous man; but I am more jealous than Sa'd; and God is still more jealous than I am." To this he further added: "Since the Sultan has made the sheykh his father, we will make some other our son." So saying, he gave his usual religious shout of ecstasy, and stalked out from the assembly.

Husāmu-'d-Dīn related that he saw the Sultan, when Jelāl thus quitted the presence, turn pale, as though shot with an arrow.

The grandees ran to stop Jelāl; but he would not return.

A few days afterwards, the officers of state adopted the resolution to invite the Sultan to go to another city, that they might take measures to get rid of Sheykh Bāba. The Sultan now went to

consult Jelāl, and ask for his blessing before setting out. Jelāl advised him not to go. The matter had, however, been officially promulgated, and there was no possibility to alter arrangements.

On arriving at the other town, the Sultan was conducted to a private apartment, and forthwith strangled with a bowstring. Ere his breath failed, he invoked the name of Jelāl.

At that moment Jelāl was at his college, lost to consciousness in the enthusiasm of a musical service. Suddenly, he put his two forefingers into his two ears, and ordered the trumpets and chorus to join in. He then shouted vociferously, and recited aloud two of his own odes, of which one commences thus:

"My words were: 'Go not; I'm thy friend; the world is rife
With threats of dire destruction; I'm the Fount of Life.'"

. . . . . .

When the service was over, the disciples requested Jelāl's son, Sultan Veled, to inquire of his father what all this might signify. In reply, he merely put off his cloak, and said aloud: "Let us perform the service for the burial of the dead."

He acted as Precentor in the service, and all present joined in. Then, without waiting for his son to put any question, he addressed the assembly, saying: "Yea, Bahā'u-'d-Dīn and my friends! They have strangled the poor Sultan Ruknu-'d-Dīn. In his agony, he called on me, and shrieked. God had so ordained. I did not wish his voice to ring in my ears, and interrupt my devotions. He will fare better in the other world."

(There is a serious anachronism in the foregoing account. Sultan Ruknu-'d-Dīn, whose name was Suleyman son of Key-Khusrew, was put to death by order of the Mogul emperor Abaqa Khān, in A.H. 664 (A.D. 1265), thirty-six years before the final extinction of the dynasty by order of Qāzān Khān, between Abaqa and whom no less than four emperors reigned. Besides this, Jelāl himself died in A.H. 672 (A.D. 1273), twenty-seven years before the last of the Seljūqī sovereigns, Key-Qubād son of Ferrāmurz son of Key-Kāwus, was slaughtered, together with all living members of the race. Historians differ much respecting the names and order of succession of the last sovereigns of the dynasty; and the present anecdote shows how confused had become on the spot the legend of these puppets. Ruknu-'d-Dīn caused his own brother to be poisoned, as he had become jealous of the favour shown to that brother by the Mogul emperor. His own death was the reward of that act.)

39.

One day, in lecturing on self-abasement and humility, Jelāl spake a parable from the trees of the field, and said: "Every tree that yields no fruit, as the pine, the cypress, the box, etc., grows tall and straight, lifting up its head on high, and sending all its branches upwards; whereas all the fruit-bearing trees droop their heads, and trail their branches. In like manner, the Apostle of God was the most humble of men. Though he carried within himself all the virtues and excellencies of the ancients and of the moderns, he, like a fruitful tree, was more humble, and more of a dervish, than any other prophet. He is related to have said: 'I am commanded to show consideration to all men, to be kind to them;

and yet, no prophet was ever so ill-treated by men as I have been.' We know that he had his head broken, and his teeth knocked out. Still he prayed: 'O our Lord God, guide Thou my people aright; for they know not what they do.' Other prophets have launched denunciations against the people to whom they were sent; and certainly, none have had greater cause to do so, than Muhammed."

"Old Adam's form was moulded first of clay from nature's face;
 Who's not, as mire, low-minded's not true son of Adam's race."

In like manner, Jelāl also had the commendable habit to show himself humble and considerate to all, even the lowest; especially so to children, and to old women. He used to bless them; and always bowed to those who bowed to him, even though these were not Muslims.

One day he met an Armenian butcher, who bowed to him seven times. Jelāl bowed to him in return. At another time he chanced upon a number of children who were playing, and who left their game, ran to him, and bowed. Jelāl bowed to them also; so much so, that one little fellow called out from afar: "Wait for me until I come." Jelāl moved not away, until the child had come, bowed, and been bowed to.

At that time, people were speaking and writing against him. Legal opinions were obtained and circulated, to the effect that music, singing, and dancing, are unlawful. Out of his kindly disposition, and love of peace, Jelāl made no reply; and after a while all his detractors were silenced, and their writings clean forgotten, as though they had never been written; whereas, his family and

followers will endure to the end of time, and will go on increasing continually.

40.

Jelāl once wrote a note to the Perwāna, interceding for a disciple who had been involved in an act of homicide, and had taken refuge in the house of another.

The Perwāna demurred; saying it was a very grave matter, a question of blood. Jelāl thereupon facetiously replied: "A homicide is popularly termed 'a son of 'Azrā'īl (the angel of death).' Being such, what on earth is he to do, unless he kill some one?"

This repartee so pleased the Perwāna, that he pardoned the culprit, and paid himself to the heirs of the slain man the price of his blood.

41.

Jelāl one day went forth and preached in the market. Crowds collected round him. But he continued until night fell around him; so he was at length left alone.

The dogs of the market-place now collected in a circle about him, wagging their tails and whining.

Seeing this, Jelāl exclaimed: "By the Lord, the Highest, the Strongest, the All-Compelling One, besides whom none is high, or strong, or powerful! These dogs comprehend my discourse, and the truths I expound. Men call them dogs; but henceforward

let them not be so termed. They are of the family of the '*Seven Sleepers*.'" (5)

42.

The Perwāna much wished Jelāl to give him private instruction at his palace; and requested Jelāl's son, Sultan Veled, to intercede for him in the matter; which he did.

Jelāl replied to his son: "Bahā'u-'d-Dīn! He cannot bear that burden." This was thrice repeated. Jelāl then remarked to his son: "Bahā'u-'d-Dīn! A bucket, the water of which is enough for forty, cannot be drained by one."

Bahā made the reflection: "Had I not pressed the matter, I had never heard this wonderful saying."

43.

At another time, the Perwāna, through Bahā'u-'d-Dīn, requested Jelāl to give a public lecture to all the men of science of the city, who were desirous to hear him.

His answer was: "A tree laden with fruit, had its branches bowed down to the earth therewith. At the time, doubts and gainsayings prevented the gardeners from gathering and enjoying the fruit. The tree has now raised its head to the skies, and beyond. Can they hope, then, to pluck and eat of its fruit?"

44.

Again, the Perwāna requested Jelāl himself to instruct him and give him counsel.

After a little reflection, Jelāl said: "I have heard that thou hast committed the Qur'ān to memory. Is it so?" "I have." "I have heard that thou hast studied, under a great teacher, the Jāmi'u-'l-Usūl, that mighty work on the 'Elements of Jurisprudence.' Is it so?" "It is."

"Then," answered Jelāl, "thou knowest the Word of God, and thou knowest all the words and acts reported of His Apostle. But thou settest them at naught, and attest not up to their precepts. How, then, canst thou expect that words of mine will profit thee?"

The Perwāna was abashed, and burst into tears. He went his way; but from that day he began to execute justice, so as to become a rival of the great Chosroes. He made himself the phœnix of the age, and Jelāl accepted him as a disciple.

45.

A company of pilgrims arrived one year at Qonya from Mekka, on their way home elsewhere. They were taken in succession to visit all the chief men of rank and learning in the capital, and were received with every demonstration of respect.

At last they were conducted to Jelāl also, in his college. On seeing him seated there, they all screamed out and fainted away.

When they were recovered, Jelāl began to offer excuses, saying to them: "I fear you have been deceived, either by an impostor, or by some person resembling me in feature. There are men who strongly resemble one another."

The pilgrims one and all objected: "Why talks he thus? Why strive to make us doubt our eyes? By the God of heaven and earth, he was with us in person, habited in the very dress he now wears, when we all assumed the pilgrim garb at Mekka. He performed with us all the ceremonies of the pilgrimage, there and at 'Arafāt. (6) He visited with us the tomb of the Prophet at Medīna; though he never once ate or drank with us. Now he pretends that he does not know us or we know him."

On hearing this declaration, Jelāl's disciples were transported with joy, a musical festival ensued, and all those pilgrims became disciples.

46.

A certain rich merchant of Qonya, a disciple, as was his wife, of Jelāl's, went to Mekka one year for the pilgrimage.

On the day when the victims are slaughtered, the lady had a dish of sweetmeat prepared, and sent some of it in a china bowl to Jelāl, to be eaten at dinner. She made the request that, when he partook of the food, he would favour her absent husband with his remembrance, his prayers, and his blessing.

Jelāl invited his disciples to the feast; and all ate of the lady's sweetmeat to repletion. But the bowl still remained full.

Jelāl then said: "Oh, he too must partake of it." He took the bowl, ascended to the terraced roof of the college with it, returning immediately empty-handed. His friends asked him what he had done with the bowl and the food. "I have handed them," said

Jelāl, "to her husband, whose property they are." The company remained bewildered.

In due course of time, the pilgrims from Qonya returned home from Mekka; and out of the baggage of the merchant, the china bowl was produced, and sent in to the lady, who was much astonished at sight of it. She inquired of her husband how he had become possessed of that identical dish. He replied: "Ah! I also am at a loss to know how it happened. But, on the eve of the slaughter of the victims, I was seated in my tent, at 'Arafāt, with a company of other pilgrims, when an arm projected into the tent, and placed this dish before me, filled with sweetmeat. I sent out servants to see who had brought it to me; but no one was found." The lady at once inferred the truth, and guessed what had happened. Her husband was more and more astonished at such miraculous power.

Next day, husband and wife went to Jelāl, stood bareheaded before him, wept for joy, and related what had occurred. He answered:

"The whole thing is the effect of your trust and belief. God has merely made use of my hand as the instrument wherewith to make manifest His power."

47.

Jelāl was accustomed to go every year for about six weeks to a place near Qonya, called *"The Hot Waters,"* where there is a lake or marsh inhabited by a large colony of frogs.

A religious musical festival was arranged one day near the lake, and Jelāl delivered a discourse. The frogs were vociferous, and made his words inaudible. He therefore addressed himself to them, with a loud shout, saying: "What is all this noise about? Either do you pronounce a discourse, or allow me to speak." Complete silence immediately ensued; nor was a frog ever once heard to croak again, so long as Jelāl remained there.

Before leaving, he went to the marsh, and gave them his permission to croak again now as much as they pleased. The chorus instantly began. Numbers of people, who were witnesses of this miraculous power over the frogs, became believers in Jelāl, and professed themselves his disciples.

48.

A party of butchers had purchased a heifer, and were leading her away to be slaughtered, when she broke loose from them, and ran away, a crowd following and shouting after her, so that she became furious, and none could pass near her.

By chance Jelāl met her, his followers being at some distance behind. On beholding him, the heifer became calm and quiet, came gently towards him, and then stood still, as though communing with him mutely, heart to heart, as is the wont with saints; and as though pleading for her life. Jelāl patted and caressed her.

The butchers now came up. Jelāl begged of them the animal's life, as having placed herself under his protection. They gave their consent, and let her go free.

Jelāl's disciples now joined the party, and he improved the occasion by the following remarks:—"If a brute beast, on being led away to slaughter, break loose and take refuge with me, so that God grants it immunity for my sake, how much more so would the case be, when a human being turns unto God with all his heart and soul, devoutly seeking Him. God will certainly save such a man from the tormenting demons of hell-fire, and lead him to heaven, there to dwell eternally."

Those words caused such joy and gladness among the disciples that a musical festival, with dancing, at once commenced, and was carried on into the night. Alms and clothing were distributed to the poor singers of the chorus.

It is related that the heifer was never seen again in the meadows of Qonya.

49.

A meeting was held at the Perwāna's palace, each guest bringing his own waxlight of about four or five pounds' weight. Jelāl came to the assembly with a small wax-taper.

The grandees smiled at the taper. Jelāl, however, told them that their imposing candles depended on his taper for their light. Their looks expressed their incredulity at this. Jelāl, therefore, blew out his taper, and all the candles were at once extinguished; the company being left in darkness.

After a short interval, Jelāl fetched a sigh. His taper took fire therefrom, and the candles all burnt brightly as before. Numerous were the conversions resulting from this miraculous display.

50.

One day, the poet-laureate, Qāni'ī, came to visit Jelāl at his college. He was the very Khāqānī (7) of the age, and was accompanied by a crowd of noble admirers.

After much conversation, Qāni'ī remarked that he did not like the writings of the poet Sanā'ī, (8) and Jelāl inquired the reason. The poet-laureate replied: "Sanā'ī was not a Muslim." Again Jelāl asked why he had formed that opinion; and Qāni'ī replied: "He has quoted passages from the Qur'ān in his poetry, and has even used them as his rhymes."

Jelāl hereupon rebuked him most severely, as follows:—

"Do hold thy peace. What sort of a Muslim art thou? Could a Muslim perceive the grandeur of that poet, his hair would stand on end, and his turban would fall from his head. That Muslim, and thousands such as he,—such as thee,—out of this lower world, and out of the land of spirits, would become real Muslims. His poetry, which is an exposition of the mysteries of the Qur'ān, is so beautifully embellished, that one may apply to it the adage: 'We have drawn from the ocean, and we have poured out again into the ocean.' Thou hast not understood his philosophy; thou hast not studied it; for thou art a Qāni'ī (Follower of one who is satisfied). The vicars of God have a technology, of which the rhetoricians have no knowledge. Hence these truths appear to be

imperfect, because men of crude minds are prevented from comprehending them. Though thou hast no part in the lot of the recondite mysteries of the saints, it does not thence follow that thou shouldest deny their position, and so place thyself in a position where destruction may be brought down upon thee. On the contrary, shouldest thou fix thy faith upon them, and act with true sincerity, thou shalt find in the day of judgment no heavy burden on thy shoulders. In lieu thereof, a burden-bearer will be present at thy side,—a refuge, who will prove thy most earnest intercessor."

Struck with these words, the poet-laureate arose, uncovered, begged forgiveness, confessed contrition for his disrespect, and became one of Jelāl's disciples.

51.

A disciple of Husāmu-'d-Dīn wished to make a vow never to do an act not expressly authorised by the Canon Law of Islām. For the purpose of administering the oath to him, instead of the Qur'ān, a copy of the Ilāhī-nāma (Divine Hymns) of the philosopher Sanā'ī was placed on a lectern, covered over with a cloth, and tendered as "the Book" on which he was to swear.

Just then, Jelāl came into the room, and asked what was going on. Husām replied: "One of my disciples is going to make a vow against backsliding. We shrank from swearing him on the Qur'ān, and have therefore prepared a copy of the Ilāhī-nāma for the occasion."

Jelāl observed: "Indeed! Why, the Ilāhī-nāma would draw down on a forswearer a more severe chastisement than the Qur'ān itself. The Word of God is but milk, of which the Ilāhī-nāma is the cream and the butter!"

52.

When Adam was created, God commanded Gabriel to take the three most precious pearls of the divine treasury, and offer them in a golden salver to Adam, to choose for himself one of the three.

The three pearls were: *wisdom, faith,* and *modesty.*

Adam chose the pearl of *wisdom.*

Gabriel then proceeded to remove the salver with the remaining two pearls, in order to replace them in the divine treasury. With all his mighty power, he found he could not lift the salver.

The two pearls said to him: "We will not separate from our beloved wisdom. We could not be happy and quiet away from it. From all eternity, we three have been the three compeers of God's glory, the pearls of His power. We cannot be separated."

A voice was now heard to proceed from the divine presence, saying: "Gabriel! leave them, and come away."

From that time, wisdom has taken its seat on the summit of the brain of Adam; faith took up its abode in his heart; modesty established itself in his countenance. Those three pearls have remained as the heirlooms of the chosen children of Adam. For,

whoever, of all his descendants, is not embellished and enriched with those three jewels, is lacking of the sentiment and lustre of his divine origin.

So runs the narrative reported by Husām, Jelāl's successor, as having been imparted to him by the latter.

53.

A certain flute-player named Hamza, much beloved by Jelāl, happened to die. Jelāl sent some of his disciples to array the defunct in his grave-clothes. He himself followed them to the house of the deceased.

On entering the room, Jelāl addresses the dead body: "My dear friend Hamza, arise!" Instantly, the deceased arose, saying: "Lo, here I am!" He then took his flute, and for three whole days and nights a religious festival was kept up in his house.

Above a hundred Roman misbelievers were thereby converted to the faith of Islām. When Jelāl left the house, life departed from the corpse also.

54.

Among the disciples there was a hunchback, a devout man, and a player on the tambourine, whom Jelāl loved.

On the occasion of a festival, this poor man beat his tambourine and shouted in ecstasy to an unusual degree. Jelāl was also greatly moved in the spirit with the holy dance.

Approaching the hunchback, he said to him: "Why erectest thou not thyself like the rest?" The infirmity of the hunch was pleaded. Jelāl then patted him on the back, and stroked him down. The poor man immediately arose, erect and graceful as a cypress.

When he went home, his wife refused him admittance, denying that he was her husband. His companions came, and bare witness to her of what had happened. Then she was convinced, let him in, and the couple lived together for many years afterwards.

55.

It was once remarked to Jelāl, with respect to the burial service for the dead, that, from the earliest times, it had been usual for certain prayers and Qur'ānic recitations to be said at the grave and round the corpse; but, that people could not understand why he had introduced into the ceremony the practice of singing hymns during the procession towards the place of burial, which canonists had pronounced to be a mischievous innovation.

Jelāl replied: "The ordinary reciters, by their services, bear witness that the deceased lived a Muslim. My singers, however, testify that he was a Muslim, a believer and a lover of God."

He added also: "Besides that; when the human spirit, after years of imprisonment in the cage and dungeon of the body, is at length set free, and wings its flight to the source whence it came, is not this an occasion for rejoicings, thanks, and dancings? The soul, in ecstasy, soars to the presence of the Eternal; and stirs up others to make proof of courage and self-sacrifice. If a prisoner be released from a dungeon and be clothed with honour, who would doubt

that rejoicings are proper? So, too, the death of a saint is an exactly parallel case."

56.

One of Jelāl's chief disciples related that, when he first began to study under that teacher, a company of pilgrims from Mekka came to Qonya, and among them was a very handsome young man of this latter city, son to one of the chief professors there.

This young man brought rich presents to Jelāl, and gifts for the disciples, relating to the latter the following adventure:—

"We were travelling in the desert of Arabia, and I chanced to fall asleep. The caravan went on without me. When I awoke, I found myself alone in the trackless sands. I knew not which way to turn. I wept and lamented for a considerable time, took a direction at hazard, and walked until I was thoroughly exhausted.

"To my surprise and joy I espied a large tent at a distance, with a great smoke rising by it. I made for the tent, and there encountered a most formidable-looking personage, to whom I related my misadventure. He bid me welcome, asked me in, and invited me to rest myself. Within the tent I observed a large kettle, full of fresh-cooked sweetmeat of the finest kind, and a plentiful supply of cool clear water.

"My wonder was great. I asked my host what these preparations might mean, and he answered: "I am a disciple of the great Jelālu-'d-Dīn of Qonya, son of Bahā'u-'d-Dīn of Balkh. He is used to pass by here every day. I have therefore pitched this tent for him, and I prepare this food. Perchance, he may honour and bless me with his presence, partaking of hospitality here.'

"As he yet spake, in walked Jelāl. We saluted; and he was begged to partake of the food. He took a little morsel, no larger than a filbert, giving me some also. I fell at his feet, and told him I was from Qonya on pilgrimage, and had missed the caravan by falling asleep. 'Well,' answered he, 'as we are fellow-townsmen, be of good cheer.' He then bade me close my eyes. I did so; and on opening them again I found myself in the midst of my companions of the caravan. I am now come here, on my return home in safety, to offer my thanks for that miraculous kindness, and to profess myself a disciple of the holy man."

57.

A man of great learning came once to visit Jelāl. By way of a test, he asked Jelāl two questions: "Is it correct to speak of God as '*a living soul*?' since God hath said (Qur'ān iii. 182): 'Every living soul shall taste death!'" and: "If one ought not to call God 'a living soul,' what did Jesus mean when he said (Qur'ān v. 116): 'Thou knowest what is in my soul, but I know not what is in Thy soul'?" The second question was: "Can God properly be called 'a thing'? If He can be so called, what is the signification of His word (Qur'ān xxviii. 88): Every thing shall perish, save His cause'?"

Jelāl immediately replied: "'But I know not what is in Thy soul' means *in Thy knowledge, in Thy absentness,* or, as we seers say, *in Thy secrecy*. Thus the passage would be paraphrased: *Thou knowest what is in my secrecy; but I know not what is in the secret of Thy secrecy;* or, as '*the people of heart*' would put it: *Thou knowest what issues from me in the world; but I know not the secret of what issues from Thee in the world to come.* It is quite proper to speak of God as 'a thing;' for He hath said (Qur'ān vi. 19): 'What thing is greatest in testimony? Say thou: "God;"' *i.e.*, God is the greatest thing in testimony; 'God will be a witness between me and you in the day of the resurrection.' The signification of the passage 'Every thing shall perish' is:*every created thing shall perish;* not the Creator, *i.e.*, 'save He.' The thing excepted from the general category is 'He: But God knows best."

The man of learning instantly professed himself a disciple, and composed a panegyric on Jelāl.

58.

The legend goes that Jelāl made a practice of seeing the new moon of the Arabian new year, and always uttered the following prayer on seeing it:—"O our Lord God! Thou art the Past-eternal One, the Future-eternal One, the Ancient One! This is a new year. I beg of Thee therein steadfastness to withstand the lapidated Satan, (9) and assistance against the rebellious spirit (within me); also, occupation in what will approximate me to Thee, and an avoidance of what might elongate me from Thee. O God! O the All-merciful One, the All-compassionate One! Through Thy mercy, O Most-compassionate of the merciful ones! O thou Lord of majesty and of honour!"

59.

It is related that Jelāl cured one of his disciples of an intermittent fever by writing down the following invocation on paper, washing off the ink in water, and giving this to the patient to drink; who was, under God's favour, immediately relieved from the malady:—"O Mother of the sleek one (a nickname of the tertian ague)! If thou hast believed in God, the Most Great, make not the head to ache; vitiate not the swallow; eat not the flesh; drink not the blood; and depart thou out of So-and-So, betaking thyself to some one who attributes to God partners of other false gods. And I bear witness that there is not any god save God, and I testify that Muhammed is His servant and apostle."

60.

One day Jelāl paid a visit to a great Sheykh. He was received with the utmost respect, and seated with the Sheykh on the same carpet, both together falling into ecstatic heart-communion with the world of spirits.

A certain dervish was there present also, who had repeatedly performed the pilgrimage at Mekka. The dervish addressed Jelāl, and inquired: "What is poverty?" Jelāl returned no answer; and the question was thrice repeated.

When Jelāl took his leave, the great Sheykh accompanied him to the street door. On his return to his room, he reprimanded the dervish severely for his insolent intrusion on the guest; "especially," said the Sheykh, "as he fully answered thy question the first time thou puttest it." The dervish, surprised, asked what the answer had been. "The poor man," said the Sheykh, "when he hath known God, hath his tongue tied. That is being a real dervish; who, when in the presence of saints, speaks not; neither with the tongue, nor with the heart. This is what is signified by

(Qur'ān xlvi. 28): 'Hold ye your peace.' But now, prepare thyself for thy end. Thou art struck by a shaft from heaven."

Three days later, the dervish was met by a gang of reprobates, who attacked and killed him, carrying off every thing he had about him. *Salve fac nos, Domine!*

61.

In the days of Jelāl there was in Qonya a lady-saint, named Fakhru-'n-Nisā (the Glory of Women). She was known to all the holy men of the time, who were all aware of her sanctity. Miracles were wrought by her in countless numbers. She constantly attended the meetings at Jelāl's home, and he occasionally paid her a visit at her house.

Her friends suggested to her that she ought to go and perform the pilgrimage at Mekka; but she would not undertake this duty unless she should first consult with Jelāl about it. Accordingly she went to see him. As she entered his presence, before she spoke, he called out to her: "Oh, most happy idea! May thy journey be prosperous! God willing, we shall be together." She bowed, but said nothing. The disciples present were puzzled.

That night she remained a guest at Jelāl's house, conversing with him till past midnight. At that hour he went up to the terraced roof of the college to perform the divine service of the vigil. When he had completed that service of worship, he fell into an ecstasy, shouting and exclaiming. Then he lifted the skylight of the room below, where the lady was, and invited her to come up on to the roof also.

When she was come, he told her to look upwards, saying that her wish was come to pass. On looking up, she beheld the Cubical House of Mekka in the air, circumambulating round Jelāl's head above him, and spinning round like a dervish in his waltz, plainly and distinctly, so as to leave no room for doubt or uncertainty. She screamed out with astonishment and fright, swooning away. On coming to herself, she felt the conviction that the journey to Mekka was not one for her to perform; so she totally relinquished the idea.

62.

Jelāl was once standing at the edge of the moat round the city of Qonya, when a company of students, undergraduates of one of the colleges in the neighbourhood, seeing him, agreed to try him by asking the question: "Of what colour was the dog of the Seven Sleepers?"

Jelāl's immediate, unpremeditated answer was: "Yellow. A lover is always yellow (sallow); as am I; and that dog was a lover." The students bowed to him, and all became disciples.

63.

The Superior of the monks of the monastery of Plato was an old man, and was held in the very highest esteem for his learning in all Constantinople and Firengistān, in Sīs, Jānik, and other lands. (Sīs was capital of the kingdom of Lower Armenia, and Jānik was the secondary "Roman Empire" of Trebizond.) From all those lands did disciples flock to learn wisdom from him.

This Superior related the following anecdote:—

"One day, Jelāl came to the monastery of Plato, situated at the foot of a hill, with a cavern therein, from whence issued a stream of cold water. Jelāl entered the cavern, and proceeded to its farther extremity. The Superior remained at the cavern's mouth, watching for what might happen. For seven whole days and nights Jelāl remained there, seated in the midst of the cold water. At the end of that period he came forth from the cavern, and walked away, singing a hymn. Not the slightest change was apparent in his features, nor in his eyes."

The Superior made oath that all he had read about the person and qualities of the Messiah, as also in the books of Abraham and Moses, were found in the person of Jelāl, as well as the grandeur and mien of the prophets, as set forth in books of ancient history, and far more besides.

64.

Shemsu-'d-Dīn of Tebrīz once asserted, in Jelāl's college, that whosoever wished to see again the prophets, had only to look on Jelāl, who possessed all their qualifications; more especially of those to whom revelations were made, whether by angelic communications, or whether in visions; the chief of such qualities being serenity of mind with perfect inward confidence and consciousness of being one of God's elect. "Now," said he, "to possess Jelāl's approbation is heaven; while hell is to incur his displeasure. Jelāl is the key of heaven. Go then, and look upon Jelāl, if thou wish to comprehend the signification of that saying *'the learned are the heirs of the prophets,'* together with something beyond that, which I will not here specify. He has more learning in every science than any one else upon earth. He explains better, with greater tact and taste, as also more exhaustively, than all others. Were I, with my mere intellect, to study for a hundred years, I could not acquire a tenth part of what he knows. He has intuitively thought out that knowledge, without being aware of it, in my presence, by his own subtlety."

65.

One of the greatest teachers of Qonya was one day giving a lecture on a terraced roof, when suddenly he heard the sound of a lute. He exclaimed: "These lutes are an innovation on the prophetic usages. They must be interdicted."

Forthwith, the form of Jelāl appeared before him, and answered: "That must not be." On this the teacher fainted away.

When he regained his consciousness, he sought to make his peace with Jelāl, by sending an apology and a recantation to him, through the medium of Jelāl's son, Sultan Veled; but Jelāl would not accept them. He answered: "It would be easier to convert seventy Roman bishops to Islām, than to clear away from the mind of that teacher the stains of hate, and so set him on the right road. His soul is as foul as the paper on which children practise their writing exercises."

At length, however, he allowed himself to be appeased by his son; so that he permitted the teacher, with his pupils, to constitute themselves his disciples.

66.

Jelāl one day addressed his son, saying: "Bahā'u-'d-Dīn, dost thou wish to love thy enemy, and to be loved of him? Speak well of him, and extol his virtues. He will then be thy friend; and for this reason: In like manner as there is a road open between the heart and the tongue, so also is there a way from the tongue to the heart. The love of God may be found by bearing His *comely names*. God hath said: 'O My servants, take ye heed that ye often commemorate Me, so that sincerity may abound.'

The more that sincerity prevails, the more do the rays of the light of truth shine into the heart. The hotter a baker's oven is, the more bread will it bake; if cool, it will not bake at all."

67.

Sultan Veled, Bahā'u-'d-Dīn, is said to have recounted of his father, Jelāl, this saying: "A true disciple is he who holds his teacher to be superior to all others. So much so, that, for instance, a disciple of Bāyezīd of Bestām was once asked whether Bāyezīd or Abū-Hanīfa was the greater, and he replied that his teacher, Bāyezīd, was the greater. 'Then,' said the questioner, 'is Bāyezīd the greater, or is Abū-Bekr?' 'My teacher is the greater.' 'Bāyezīd or Muhammed?' 'Bāyezīd.' 'Bāyezīd or God?' 'I only know my teacher; I know no other than him; and I know that he is greater than all others.'

"Another was asked the last question, and his reply was: 'There is no difference between the two.' A third was asked it also, and he replied: 'It would require a greater one than either of the two to determine which of them is the greater.'

"As God does not walk in this world of sensible objects, the prophets are the substitutes of God. No, no! I am wrong! For if thou suppose that those substitutes and their principal are two different things, thou hast judged erroneously, not rightly."

68.

Sultan Veled is reported to have said: "My grandfather, the Great Master, used to recommend to his disciples to honour his son Jelāl exceedingly, as one of noble extraction and exalted pedigree, of an eternal descent in the past; since the mother of his mother was the daughter of the Imām Sarakhsī, a descendant from Huseyn, son of 'Alī, and grandson of the Prophet."

69.

Sultan Veled is also reported to have said: "My father told his disciples that I was seven, and my brother 'Alā'u-'d-Dīn eight years old, when the Dizdār Bedru-'d-Dīn Guhertāsh had us circumcised at Qara-Hisār." (See chap. I., No. 12.)

He is also reported to have declared: "When the Sultan invited my grandfather to Qonya, a year passed, and then the Emīr Mūsa invited my grandfather to Larenda, and took my father to be his own son-in-law; so that I was born in that town." (See chap. I., No. 2. The account now given here is at variance with that mentioned in the preface, which makes 'Alā'u-'d-Dīn and Bahā'u-'d-Dīn to have been born at Larenda before Jelāl and his father went to Qonya. Moreover, their mother, Gevher Khātūn, is there said to have been the daughter of Lala Sherefu-'d-Dīn of Samarqand. Is that an alias of the Emīr Mūsa of the present anecdote; or did Jelāl marry two ladies of Larenda at different times? There are several difficulties here. Sultan Veled puts only one year as the difference of age between himself and his elder brother. If the daughter of the Emīr Mūsa was the mother of both these brothers, Jelāl's stay at Larenda must have been of about two years at least. If they were by different mothers, and born, the one before, the other after Bahā Veled's settling at Qonya, there must have been a greater difference in their ages. Jelāl's age at his marriage is also variously stated. These discrepancies show that the anecdotes were collected from traditions of various sources, long after the events recorded.)

70.

Sultan Veled is said to have related that one day, two Turks, law-students, brought to Jelāl an offering of a few lentils, excusing the paucity of the gift, as the result of their poverty. Jelāl thereupon narrated the following anecdote:—

"God revealed to Mustafa (Muhammed) that the believers should contribute of their possessions, for the service of God, as much as they could spare. Some brought the half, some the third part; Abū-Bekr brought the whole of what he possessed. Thus a large treasure was collected, of money, beasts, and arms, for God's service.

"A poor woman, too, brought three dates and a cake of bread—all she had on earth.

"The disciples smiled. Mustafa perceived their action, and said that God had showed him a vision, which he desired to tell to them. They all begged he would favour them with the recital. He therefore thus proceeded:

"'God hath removed the veils from before me. And lo, I saw that the angels had placed in one scale of a balance the whole of your very liberal offerings together, and in the other scale the three dates and one cake of this poor woman. The latter scale was preponderant; its contents outweighed all the rest.'

"The disciples bowed, thanked the prophet; and inquired the hidden explanation of this mystery. He answered: 'This poor woman has parted with her all, whereas my disciples have kept back a part of their possessions. Proverbs say: "The generous one is generous out of what he possesses," and, "A little, in the eyes of the Most Great, is much." You put into the earth a single date-stone, intrusting it to God. He makes that stone become a tree, which yields fruits without number; because the stone was confided to Him. Therefore, let your alms be given to the poor, and to God's servants, as a trust committed unto God. For it is said: "Alms fall first into God's hand, before reaching the hands of the poor;" and again: "Alms for the poor and the destitute."'

"The poor of Mekka and Medīna, refugees and auxiliaries, shouted their admiration as they heard these words."

When the two Turkish students heard this anecdote related, they professed themselves disciples of Jelāl.

71.

When Jelāl was quite young, he was one day preaching on the subject of Moses and Elias (Qur'ān xviii. 59-81). One of his disciples noticed a stranger seated in a corner, paying great attention, and every now and then saying: "Good! Quite true! Quite correct! He might have been the third one with us two!" The disciple surmised that the stranger might be Elias. (Elias is believed by Muslims to be always visible somewhere, but that people know him not. Did they recognise him, they could obtain from him a knowledge of the secret of eternal life, which he possesses.) He therefore seized hold of the stranger's skirt, and asked for his spiritual aid. "Oh," said the stranger, "rather seek assistance from Jelāl, as we all do. Every occult saint of God is the loving and admiring friend of him." So saying, he managed to disengage his skirt from the disciple's hold, and instantly disappeared. The disciple went to pay his respects to Jelāl, who at once addressed him, saying: "Elias, and Moses, and the prophets, are all friends of mine." The disciple understood the allusion, and became more and more devoted at heart to Jelāl than he even was before.

72.

It is related that when the burial service was about to be performed over the corpse of Jelāl, the precentor gave a shriek, and swooned away. After a while, he recovered, and then performed his office, weeping bitterly.

On being asked the cause of his emotion, he answered: "As I stood forward to perform my office, I perceived a row of the most noble of spiritual saints of the spiritual world, as being present, and as being engaged in reciting the prayers for the dead over the departed one. Those angels of heaven wore robes of blue (the mourning of some sects of Muslims), and wept."

For forty days, that precentor and others daily visited Jelāl's grave.

73.

At Damascus, when a young student, Jelāl was frequently seen by others to walk several arrow-flights' distance in the air, tranquilly returning to the terraced roof on which they were standing.

Those fellow-pupils were among his earliest believers and disciples.

74.

A friend of Jelāl's once took leave of him at Qonya, and went to Damascus. On his arrival there, he found Jelāl seated in a corner of his room. Asking for an explanation of this surprising phenomenon, Jelāl replied: "The men of God are like fishes in the ocean; they pop up into view on the surface here and there and everywhere, as they please."

75.

Jelāl once met a Turk in Qonya, who was selling fox-skins in the market, and crying them: "Dilku! Dilku!" (Fox! Fox! in Turkish.)

Jelāl immediately began to parody his cry, calling out in Persian: "Dil kū! Dil kū!" (Heart, where art thou?) At the same time he broke out into one of his holy waltzes of ecstasy.

76.

In the time of Sultan Veled (A.D. 1284-1312), a young man, of the descendants of the Prophet, and son of the guardian of the holy tomb of Muhammed at Medīna, came to Qonya with a company of his fellow-descendants, belonging to that city. He was presented to Sultan Veled, and became his disciple.

He wore a most singular head-dress. One end of his turban hung down in front to below his navel; while the other end was formed into the *sheker-āvīz* (10) of the Mevlevi dervishes.

When they had become somewhat intimate, Sultan Veled asked him how it happened that he wore the *sheker-āvīz* of the Mevlevis, when nobody else but those dervishes wear it, in imitation of their founder, Jelāl.

The young man explained that his family were descended from the Prophet. That the Prophet, on the night of his ascension to heaven, after seeing God and many mysteries, had returned a certain distance, and, as is well known, then went back to intercede with God for his people. He now perceived, on the pinnacle of God's throne, the ideal portrait of a form, so beautiful, that he had not hitherto witnessed anything so charming among the angels and inhabitants of heaven.

After contemplating the lovely vision, in amazement, for some time, Muhammed was able to notice that the ideal form wore on its head a *sheker-āvīz*. He asked Gabriel what that ideal portrait might portend, which was so attractive in its beauty as to surpass all the wonders he had witnessed in all the nine heavens. "Is it the

portrait of an angel, a prophet, or a saint?" Gabriel replied: "It is the portrait of a personage of the descendants of Abū-Bekr, who will appear in the latter days among the people of thy Church, and will fill the whole world with the effulgence of the knowledge of thy mysteries. To him will God vouchsafe a precedency, and a pen, and a breath, such that kings and princes will profess themselves his disciples; and he will be a most pure upholder of thy religion, being, in every respect, the counterpart of thyself in aspect and in morals. His name will be Muhammed, as is thine; and his surname will be Jelālu-'d-Dīn. His words will explain thy sayings, and will expound thy Qur'ān."

On his return home, the Prophet adopted the form of turban he had seen worn in that ideal portrait, making one end hang down a span in front, and binding the other end behind into a *sheker-āvīz*.

"From that day to this," said the young man, "the fathers of our family have followed that fashion, so adopted by the Prophet; and we continue to do so too."

It is said that when Abū-Bekr heard this narrative from the Prophet, respecting his great descendant that was thus foretold, he gave the whole of his possessions to the Prophet, to be expended in God's cause.

When Muhammed died, Abū-Bekr wept long and bitterly. But the Prophet appeared to him, and consoled him by saying: "One day I will reappear among my people from out of the collar of one of thy race."

The young man continued: "From that time onwards, our family were on the outlook for the manifestation of the holy personage whose ideal portrait the Prophet so saw. Thank God that I have witnessed the realisation of their hope."

The Qonya pilgrims published this communication to all the disciples there present.

77.

In the days of Sultan Veled, a great merchant came to Qonya to visit the tomb of Jelāl. He offered many rich gifts to Sultan Veled, making presents also to the disciples. He related to them many anecdotes of adventures encountered by him in his travels, such as the following:—

He once went to Kīsh and Bahreyn in quest of pearls and rubies. "An inhabitant told me," said he, "that I should find some in the hands of a certain fisherman. I went to him, and the fisher showed me a chest, containing pearls of inestimable value, such as impressed me with astonishment. I asked him how he had collected them; and he told me, calling God to witness, that he, his three brothers, and his father, were formerly poor fishermen. One day they hooked something that gave them immense trouble before they could bring it to land.

"They now found they had captured a 'Lord of the Waters,' also named a 'Marvel of the Sea,' as is commonly known. (11)

"We wondered," said he, "what we could do with the beast. We wept for the ill fortune that had brought us such a

disappointment. The creature looked at us as we spoke. Suddenly my father cried out: 'I have it! I will put him on a cart, and exhibit him all over the country at a penny a head!'

"Through the miraculous power of Him who has endowed man with speech and His creatures with life, the beast broke forth and exclaimed: 'Make me not a staring-block in the world, and I will do anything you may wish of me, so as to suffice for you and your children for many years to come!'

"Our father answered: 'How should I set thee free, when thou art so strange and unparalleled a creature?' The beast replied: 'I will make an oath.' Our father said: 'Speak! Let us hear thy oath.'

"The beast now said: 'We are of the faith of Muhammed, and disciples of the holy Mevlānā. By the soul of the Mevlānā, the holy Jelālu-'d-Dīn of Rome, I will go, and I will return.'

"Our father fainted away with astonishment. I, therefore, now asked: 'How hast thou any knowledge of him?' The beast replied: 'We are a nation of twelve thousand individuals. We have believed in him, and he frequently showed himself to us at the bottom of the sea, lecturing and sermonising to us on the divine mysteries of the truth. He brought us to a knowledge of the true faith; so that we continually practise what he taught us.'

"Our father instantly told him he was free. He went back, therefore, into the water, and was lost to sight. But two days later he returned, and brought with him innumerable pearls and precious stones. He asked whether he had been true and faithful

to his promise; and on our expressing our satisfaction on that score, he took an affectionate farewell from us.

"We were thus raised from the depths of poverty to the pinnacle of wealth. We became merchant princes, and our slaves are the great merchants of the earth. Every dealer who wishes for pearls and rubies comes to us. We are known as the *Sons of the Fisherman*. Our father went to Qonya, and paid his respects to the Mevlānā.

"Through his narrative, I formed the design, now carried into effect, to visit the son of that great saint."

This wonderful narrative has been handed down ever since in the mouths of the merchants of Qonya.

78.

(The following appears to be an account of one of the first visits of the Perwāna to Jelāl, to whom he subsequently became so devotedly attached.)

One of the most eminent among the men of learning in Qonya was visited by the Perwāna. The learned man held forth eloquently on several exalted themes, and then informed the Perwāna that he had, the night before, been taken up into the highest heaven, and had there learnt many mysteries. He said that he there saw Jelāl hold a higher station of proximity to God than any other saint, as he stood on a level with God's throne.

A day or two later, the Perwāna, filled with reverence for Jelāl's unequalled sanctity, went and paid him a visit with the utmost deference. Before the Perwāna could broach any subject of

conversation, Jelāl said to him: "Mu'īnu-'d-Dīn! the vision related to you by your learned friend is quite true in the main facts, though I never saw him there at any time." He then extemporised the following ode:—

"Fellow-visitant wert thou? Then say what thou sawest there last night.
'Twixt my heart and inspiring loved darling what passed in thy sight?
And if thou, in thy dream, with thy eyes sawest my beautiful love,
Tell us then, in the earrings he wore there what jewels were wove.
If with me thou be fellow in coat, as in thoughts and in creeds,
Let us hear the details of that ragged old mendicant's weeds.
If thou poverty's son be, and unspoken mysteries hear,
Thou'lt recount all the words that were thought by my silent compeer,
If thou'st learnt whence the source of mankind and of souls did proceed.
Since the source was but one, what then means all this search, all this greed?
And if thou hast not seen any place of his form and face free,
Say then what, in the thoughts of his lovers, that face and form be.
And if I head the lists of those lovers, as thou seemest to say,
Tell us, What are those lists? What his messages, words, answers? Pray!"

A musical service was then got up, this ode being chanted during its performance. The Perwāna was so utterly bewildered by this

incident, that he could say nothing. He therefore rose, bowed, and took his leave.

79.

One day, it is said, the Prophet (Muhammed) recited to 'Alī in private the secrets and mysteries of the "Brethren of Sincerity" (who appear to be the "Freemasons" of the Muslim dervish world), enjoining on him not to divulge them to any of the uninitiated, so that they should not be betrayed; also, to yield obedience to the rule of implicit submission.

For forty days, 'Alī kept the secret in his own sole breast, and bore therewith until he was sick at heart. Like a pregnant woman, his abdomen became swollen with the burden, so that he could no longer breathe freely.

He therefore fled to the open wilderness, and there chanced upon a well. He stooped, reached his head as far down into the well as he was able; and then, one by one, he confided those mysteries to the bowels of the earth. From the excess of his excitement, his mouth filled with froth and foam. These he spat out into the water of the well, until he had freed himself of the whole, and he felt relieved.

After a certain number of days, a single reed was observed to be growing in that well. It waxed and shot up, until at length a youth, whose heart was miraculously enlightened on the point, became aware of this growing plant, cut it down, drilled holes in it, and began to play upon it airs, similar to those performed by the

dervish lovers of God, as he pastured his sheep in the neighbourhood.

By degrees, the various tribes of Arabs of the desert heard of this flute-playing of the shepherd, and its fame spread abroad. The camels and the sheep of the whole region would gather around him as he piped, ceasing to pasture that they might listen. From all directions, north and south, the nomads flocked to hear his strains, going into ecstasies with delight, weeping for joy and pleasure, breaking forth in transports of gratification.

The rumour at length reached the ears of the Prophet, who gave orders for the piper to be brought before him. When he began to play in the sacred presence, all the holy disciples of God's messenger were moved to tears and transports, bursting forth with shouts and exclamations of pure bliss, and losing all consciousness. The Prophet declared that the notes of the shepherd's flute were the interpretation of the holy mysteries he had confided in private to 'Alī's charge. (12)

Thus it is that, until a man acquire the sincere devotion of the linnet-voiced flute-reed, he cannot hear the mysteries of the Brethren of Sincerity in its dulcet notes, or realise the delights thereof; for "faith is altogether a yearning of the heart, and a gratification of the spiritual sense."

"To whom, alas, the pangs my love for thee excites, to breathe?
My sighs, like 'Alī, I'll to some deep well's recess bequeathe.
Perchance some reeds may spring therefrom, its brink to overgrow;
Those reeds may moaning flutes become, and so betray my woe.

Who hear will say: 'Be silent, flutes! We're not love's confidants;
To that sweet tyrant make excuse for us and for those plants!'"

80.

One of Jelāl's disciples possessed a slave girl of Roman origin, whom Jelāl had named Siddīqa (after Muhammed's virgin wife 'Ā'isha). Occasionally she had miraculous visions. She used to see aureolas of heavenly light, green, red, and *black*. Various of the angels used to visit her, and souls of the departed.

Her master was vexed at her being so favoured above himself. Once he was visited by Jelāl, and expressed his chagrin to him on the subject. Jelāl replied: "True! There is a heavenly light resides in the pupils of some eyes. These occasionally mislead a few with visions of beauteous form, with which they fall in love. Others they preserve in chastity, and lead them to their adored Maker. Others, again, they may lead to take delight in exterior objects, so as to cast their eyes on every pretty face they see, while the wife at home is curtained away from her husband. Thus, whenever God opens a way to any one, appearing to him, and showing him glimpses of the hidden world, he is apt to become entranced therewith, and to lose all power of further progress, saying to himself: 'How greatly in favour am I!' Others, in short, use every endeavour; but nothing is vouchsafed to them in visions, until they be favoured with a special sight of God Himself, and they be admitted to a near approach unto Him."

The girl's master was comforted, and bowed to his teacher, whose disciples then broke out into a holy service of psalmody and dancing.

81.

There was once a wise monk in the monastery of Plato, who was on very friendly terms with Jelāl's grandson 'Ārif. He was very aged, and used to be visited by the dervishes of his neighbourhood, to whom he was very polite, and towards whom he exhibited great confidence; so much so that, one day, some of them inquired of him how he had found Jelāl, and what he had thought of him.

The monk replied to them: "What do you know of him, as to who or what he was? I have seen signs and miracles without number worked by him. I became his devoted servant. I had read in the gospel and in the prophets the lives and the works of the saints of old, and I saw that he compassed them all. I therefore had faith in the truth of his reality.

"One day he came here, conferring on me the honour of a visit. For forty days he shut himself up in ecstatic seclusion. When at length he came forth from his privacy, I laid hold of his skirt, and said to him: 'God, in His holy scripture hath said (Qur'ān xix. 72): "And there is none of you but shall come to it (hellfire)." Now, since it is incontestable that all shall come to the fire of hell, what preference is there in Islām over our faith?'

"For a little time he made no answer. At length, however, he made a sign towards the city, and went away in that direction. I followed after him leisurely. Near the city, we came to a bakehouse, the oven of which was being heated. He now took my black cassock, wrapped it in his own cloak, and threw the bundle into the oven. He then withdrew for a time into a corner, sunk in meditation.

"I saw a great smoke come out of the oven, such that no one had the power of utterance. After that, he said to me: 'Behold!' The baker withdrew the bundle from the oven, and assisted the saint to put on his cloak, which had become exquisitely clean; whereas my cassock was, as it were, branded and scorched, so as to fall in pieces. Then he said: 'Thus shall we enter therein, and thus shall you enter!'

"That self-same moment I made my bow to him and became his disciple."

82.

The reason why the Mesnevī was written is related to have been the following:—

Husāmu-'d-Dīn learnt that several of the followers of Jelāl were fond of studying the Ilāhī-nāma of Senā'ī, the Hakīm, and the Mantiqu-'t-Tayr of 'Attār, as also the Nasīb-nāma of the latter.

He therefore sought and found an opportunity to propose that Jelāl should indite something in the style of the Ilāhī-nāma, but in the metre of the Mantiqu-'t-Tayr; saying that the circle of friends would then willingly give up all other poetry, and study that alone.

Jelāl immediately produced a portion of the Mesnevī, saying that God had forewarned him of the wishes of the brethren, in consequence of which he had already begun to compose the work. That fragment consisted of the first eighteen couplets of the introductory verses

"From reed-flute hear what tale it tells,
 What plaint it makes of absence' ills," etc.

It is of the metre *Remel*, hexameter contracted:

Jelāl frequently mentions Husām as the cause of the work's having been begun and continued. In the fourth book he addresses him in the opening couplet:

"Of Truth, the light; of Faith, the sword; Husāmu-'d-Dīn aye be;
 Above the lunar orb has clomb my Mesnevī, through thee."

And again the sixth book has for its opening verse the following apostrophe:—

"O thou, Husāmu-'d-Dīn, my heart's true life! Zeal, for thy sake,
 I feel springs up in me sixth book hereby to undertake."

Often they spent whole nights at the task, Jelāl inditing, and Husām writing down his inspirations, chanting it aloud, as he wrote it, with his beautiful voice. Just as the first book was completed, Husām's wife died, and an interval ensued.

Two years thus passed without progress. Husām married again; and in that year, A.H. 662 (A.D. 1263), the second book was commenced. No other interval occurred until the work was brought to a conclusion. The third couplet of the second book mentions Husām in these terms—

"When thou, of Truth the light, Husāmu-'d-Dīn, thy courser's rein

Didst turn, descending earthward from the zenith's starry plain."

The third, fifth, and seventh books have similar addresses to Husām in their opening verses. His name is also mentioned cursorily in the third tale of the first book.

83.

On the death of Jelāl, a party of zealots went in a body to the Perwāna, explaining to him that the new practices of music and dancing, introduced by Jelāl, were innovations altogether contrary to the canonical institutes, and begging him to use his utmost endeavours to suppress them.

The Perwāna called on the learned Mufti of Qonya, Sheykh Sadru-'d-Dīn, and consulted him on the subject. The Mufti's answer was: "Do nothing of the kind. Listen not to such biased suggestions. There is an apostolical saying to this effect: 'A laudable innovation, introduced by a perfect follower of the prophets, is of the same nature with the customary practices of the prophets themselves.'" The Perwāna resolved, therefore, to do nothing towards suppressing Jelāl's institutions.

84.

A certain great man, who esteemed Jelāl, was nevertheless shocked that he should, with all his learning and piety, sanction the use of music and dancing.

He had occasion to visit Jelāl, who at once addressed him as follows:—"It is an axiom in the sacred canons that a Muslim, if hard pressed, and in danger of death, may eat of carrion and other forbidden food, so that the life of a man be not sacrificed. This rule is admitted and approved by all the authorities of the law. Now, we *men of God* are exactly in that position of extreme danger to our lives; and from that danger there is no escape, save by song, by music, and by the dance. Otherwise, through the awful majesty of the divine manifestations, the bodies of the saints would melt away as wax, and disappear like snow under the beams of a July sun."

The personage thus addressed was so struck with the earnestness of Jelāl's manner, and the cogency of his reasoning, that he became convinced, and thenceforward was a defender and upholder of Jelāl's institutions, so that these formed, as it were, the very nourishment of his heart. Many of the learned followed his example, and joined themselves to Jelāl's followers and disciples.

85.

Kālūmān and 'Aynu-'d-Devla were two Roman painters. They were unrivalled in their art of painting portraits and pictures. Both were disciples of Jelāl.

Kālūmān one day narrated that in Constantinople, on a certain tablet, the portraits of the Lady Meryem and of Jesus were painted, in such style as to be matchless. From all parts of the world artists came and tried their best; but none could produce the equal of those two portraits.

'Aynu-'d-Devla undertook, therefore, to journey to Constantinople, and see this picture. He made himself an inmate of the great church of Constantinople for a whole year, and served the priests thereof in various ways.

One night, then, he spied his opportunity, took the tablet under his arm, and absconded with it.

On reaching Qonya, he paid his respects to Jelāl, who inquired of him where he had been. He narrated to Jelāl all that had occurred with the tablet, which he exhibited.

Jelāl found the picture exceedingly beautiful, and gazed on it long with the utmost pleasure. He then spake as follows

"These two beautiful portraits complain of you, saying that you are not a faithful admirer of theirs, but are an untrue lover." The artist asked: "How?" Jelāl replied: "They say they are not supplied with food and rest. On the contrary, they are kept sleepless every night, and fasting every day. They complain: 'Aynu-'d-Devla leaves us, sleeps himself all night, and takes his meals by day, never remaining with us to do as we do!'"

The artist remarked: "Food and sleep are to them impossibilities. Neither have they speech, with which to say anything. They are mere lifeless effigies."

Jelāl now replied: "Thou art a living effigy. Thou hast acquired a knowledge of various arts. Thou art the handiwork of a limner whose hand has framed the universe, the human race, and all things on earth and in heaven. Is it right that thou forsake Him, and enamour thyself of an insignificant lifeless effigy? What profit is there in these portraits? What advantage can accrue to thee from them?"

Touched by these reproaches, the artist vowed repentance of his sin, and professed himself a Muslim.

86.

When the time of Jelāl's death drew near, he cautioned his disciples to have no fear or anxiety on that account; for," said he, "as the spirit of Mansūr (13) appeared, a hundred and fifty years after his death, to the Sheykh Ferīdu-'d-Dīn 'Attār, and became the Sheykh's spiritual guide and teacher, so, too, do you always be with me, whatever may happen, and remember me, so that I may show myself to you, in whatever form that may be;—that I may always belong to you, and ever be shedding in your breasts the light of heavenly inspiration. I will simply remind you now that our dear Lord, Muhammed, the Apostle of God, said to his disciples: 'My life is a blessing unto you, and my death will be a blessing unto you. In my life I have guided you, and after my death I will send blessings on you.'"

Jelāl's friends shed tears all, and broke out into sighs and lamentations; but bowed their heads in reverence.

It is said that he gave directions to get ready his grave-clothes, and that his wife, Kirā Khātūn, began to wail, tearing her clothes, and exclaiming: "O thou light of the world, life of the human race; unto whom wilt thou commit us? Whither wilt thou go?"

He answered her: "Whither will I go? Verily, I shall not quit your circle." She then asked: "Will there be another like unto thee, our Lord? Will another become manifest?" He replied: "If there be, he will be I." After a while he added: "While in the body, I have two attachments; one, to you; the other, to the flesh. When, by the grace of the unique Spirit, I become disembodied,—when the world of unbodied spirits, unity, and singleness, shall appear, my attachment to the flesh will become attachment to you, and I shall then have but one sole attachment."

87.

With his last breath Jelāl recommended to Husāmu-'d-Dīn to lay him in the upper part of his tomb, so that he might be the first to rise at the last day.

As he lay in his extreme sickness, there were earthquakes for seven days and nights, very severe, so that walls and houses were overthrown. On the seventh occasion, all his disciples were alarmed. He, however, calmly remarked: "Poor earth! It is eager for a fat morsel! It shall have one!"

He then gave his last instructions to his disciples, as follows:—"I recommend unto you the fear of God, in public and in private; abstemiousness in eating and in sleeping, as also in speaking; the avoidance of rebelliousness and of sin; constancy in fasting, continuous worship, and perpetual abstinence from fleshly lusts; long-suffering under the ill-treatment of all mankind; to shun the companionship of the light-minded and of the common herd; to associate with the righteous and with men of worth. For verily *'the best of mankind is he who benefiteth men,'* (14) and *'the best of speech is that which is short and to the purpose.'*" (15)

88.

The following is a prayer taught by Jelāl, on his deathbed, to one of his friends, to be used whenever affliction or care might weigh upon him:—

"O our Lord God, I breathe but for Thee, and I stretch forth my spirit towards Thee, that I may recite Thy doxologies abundantly, commemorating Thee frequently. O our Lord God, lay not on me an ailment that may make me forgetful to commemorate Thee, or lessen my yearning towards Thee, or cut off the delight I experience in reciting the litanies of Thy praise. Grant me not a health that may engender or increase in me presumptuous or thankless insolence. For Thy mercy's sake, O Thou Most-Merciful of the compassionate. Amen."

89.

A friend was seated by Jelāl's pillow, and Jelāl leaned on that friend's bosom. Suddenly a most handsome youth appeared at the door of the room, to the utmost astonishment of the friend.

Jelāl arose and advanced to receive the stranger. But the friend was quicker, and quietly asked his business. The stranger answered: "I am 'Azrā'īl, the angel of departure and separation. I am come, by the divine command, to inquire what commission the Master may have to intrust to me."

Blessed are the eyes that can perceive such sights!

The friend was near fainting at this answer. But he heard Jelāl call out: "Come in, come in, thou messenger of my King. Do that which thou art bidden; and, God willing, thou shalt find me one of the patient."

He now told his attendants to bring a vessel of water, placed his two feet therein, and occasionally sprinkled a little on his breast and forehead, saying: "My beloved (God) has proffered me a cup of poison (bitterness). From his hand I drink that poison with delight."

The singers and musicians now came in, and executed a hymn, while the whole company of friends wept, and sobbed loudly.

Jelāl observed: "It is as my friends say. But, were they even to pull down the house, what use? See my panting heart; look at my delight. The sun sheds a grateful light on the moth. My friends invite me one way; my teacher Shemsu-'d-Dīn beckons me the other way. Comply ye with the summoner of the Lord, and have faith in Him. Departure is inevitable. All being came out of nothing, and again it will be shut up in the prison of nullity. Such is God's decree from all eternity; and, to decree belongeth unto God, the Most High, the All-Great!"

His son Sultan Veled had been unremitting in his attentions. He wept and sobbed. He was reduced to a shadow. Jelāl therefore said to him: "Bahā'u-'d-Dīn, my son, I am better. Go and lie down a little. Rest thyself, and sleep awhile!"

When he was gone, Jelāl indited his last ode; thus:—

"Go! head on pillow lay; alone, in peace, me leave,
Loved tyrant, plague by night, while all around thee grieve.
That peerless beauty (God) has no need kind care to show;
But, sallow lovers, ye must patient faith still know.
Perplexity is ours to bear; 'tis his to own hard heart;
Shed he our blood; what sin? He'll not pay murder's smart.
To die's hard, after all; but remedy there's none;
How, then, to crave a remedy? The evil's done.
Last night, in dream, a warder, from my love's abode,
Made sign to me, and said: 'This way! Hold thou my lode.'"

. . . . . .

90.

It is related that, after his death, when laid on his bier, and while he was being washed by the hands of a loving and beloved disciple, while others poured the water for the ablution of Jelāl's

body, not one drop was allowed to fall to the earth. All was caught by the fond ones around, as had been the case with the Prophet at his death. Every drop was drunk by them as the holiest and purest of waters.

As the washer folded Jelāl's arms over his breast, a tremor appeared to pass over the corpse, and the washer fell with his face on the lifeless breast, weeping. He felt his ear pulled by the dead saint's hand, as an admonition. On this, he fainted away, and in his swoon he heard a cry from heaven, which said to him: "Ho there! Verily the saints of the Lord have nothing to fear, neither shall they sorrow. Believers die not; they merely depart from one habitation to another abode!"

91.

When the corpse was brought forth, all the men, women, and children, who flocked to the funeral procession, smote their breasts, rent their garments, and uttered loud lamentations. These mourners were of all creeds, and of various nations; Jews and Christians, Turks, Romans, and Arabians were among them. Each recited sacred passages, according to their several usages, from the Law, the Psalms, or the Gospel.

The Muslims strove to drive away these strangers, with blows of fist, or staff, or sword. They would not be repelled. A great tumult was the result. The Sultan, the Heir-Apparent, and the Perwāna all flew to appease the strife, together with the chief Rabbis, the Bishops, Abbots, etc.

It was asked of these latter why they mixed themselves up with the funeral of an eminent Muslim sage and saint. They replied that they had learnt from him more of the mysteries shrouded in their scriptures, than they had ever known before; and had found in him all the signs and qualities of a prophet and saint, as set forth in those writings. They further declared: "If you Muslims hold him to have been the Muhammed of his age, we esteem him as the Moses, the David, the Jesus of our time; and we are his disciples, his adherents."

The Muslim leaders could make no answer. And so, in all honour, with every possible demonstration of love and respect, was he borne along, and at length laid in his grave.

He had died as the sun went down, on Sunday, the fifth of the month Jumāda-'l-ākhir, A.H. 672 (16th December A.D. 1273); being thus sixty-eight (lunar) years (sixty-six solar years) of age.

92.

Sultan Veled is reported to have related that, shortly after the death of his father, Jelāl, he was sitting with his step-mother, Jelāl's widow, Kirā Khātūn, and Husāmu-'d-Dīn, when his step-mother saw the spirit of the departed saint, winged as a seraph, poised over his, Sultan Veled's, head, to watch over him.

93.

Jelāl had a female disciple, a saint, named Nizāma Khātūn, an intimate friend of his wife's.

Nizāma formed the design to give a spiritual party to Jelāl, with an entertainment for his disciples. She possessed nothing but a Thevr (*or* Sevr) (16) veil, which she had destined to be her own winding-sheet.

She now ordered her servants to sell this veil, and so procure the necessaries for the projected feast. But, that same morning, Jelāl came to her house with his disciples, and, addressing her, said: "Nizāma Khātūn, sell not thy veil; to thee it is a piece of necessary furniture. Lo! We are come to thy entertainment."

He and his disciples remained with her, engaged in spiritual exercises, three whole days and nights.

94.

After Jelāl's death, Kīgātū Khān, a Mogul general, came up against Qonya, intending to sack the city and massacre the inhabitants. (He was emperor from A.H. 690 to 696, A.D. 1290-1294.)

That night, in a dream, he saw Jelāl, who seized him by the throat, and nearly choked him, saying to him: "Qonya is mine. What seekest thou from its people?"

On awaking from his dream, he fell on his knees and prayed for mercy, seeking also for information as to what that portent might signify. He sent in an ambassador to beg permission for him to enter the city as a friendly guest.

When he arrived at the palace, the nobles of Qonya flocked to his court with rich offerings. All being seated in solemn conclave, Kīgātū was suddenly seized with a violent tremor, and asked one

of the princes of the city, who was seated on a sofa by himself: "Who may the personage be that is sitting at your side on your sofa?" The prince looked about, right and left; but saw no one. He replied accordingly. Kīgātū answered: "What? How sayest thou? I see by thy side, seated, a tall man with a grisly beard and a sallow complexion, a grey turban, and an Indian plaid over his chest, who looks at me most pryingly."

The prince sagaciously suspected forthwith that Jelāl's shade was there present by his side, and made answer: "The sacred eyes of majesty alone are privileged to witness that vision. It is the son of Bahā'u-'d-Dīn of Balkh, our Lord Jelālu-'d-Dīn, who is entombed in this land."

The Khān replied: "Last night I saw him in my dream. He went nigh choking me, and told me Qonya is his possession. Now, prince, thee I call my adoptive father; and I entirely forego my intention to devastate this city. Tell me; has that holy man any son or descendant alive here?"

The prince told him of Bahā Veled, now Sheykh of the city, and the peerless saint of God. Kīgātū expressed the wish to go and visit the Sheykh. The prince conducted him and his suite of nobles to Sultan Veled. They all declared themselves his disciples, and assumed the dervish turban. Bahā recounted to the Khān the history of his grandfather's expulsion from Balkh, and of all that followed. The Khān offered him royal presents, and accompanied him on a visit of reverence to the shrine of the deceased saint.

Footnotes

1. The truly eminent author of the Mesnevī.

2. From the city of Sarakhs in Khurāsān.

3. Had Dr. Tanner, the forty days' faster at New York, heard of these performances?

4. As related of certain Sabbath-breaking Jews, in Qur'ān ii. 61.

5. Qur'ān xviii. 8, etc.

6. The mount where the victims are slaughtered by the pilgrims.

7. The great Persian poet Khāqānī, born at Shirwān, died and was buried at Tebrīz A.H. 582 (A.D. 1186).

8. Sanā'ī, of Gazna in Afgānistān, surnamed "the Wise," or "the Philosopher," died and was buried at the place of his birth, A.H. 576 (A.D. 1180).

9. "*Satan, the Lapidated One*," is the chief title of the accursed one. Muslims believe that the "shooting stars" are missiles cast by angels at demons who attempt to approach heaven for eavesdropping purposes.

10. I have not met with an explanation of this word in any Persian dictionary. Literally it signifies *sugar-hanging*. In the Bahāri-'Ajem alone is it mentioned, with a distich from Hāfiz; but it is left unexplained.

11. Apparently a "*merman*" is intended.

12. This is a much more poetical account of the origin of the reed-flute than the pagan Greek myths of Orpheus and his lyre, Pan and his pipe, for which no reasons are assigned.

13. Mansūr, son of 'Ammār, thus mentioned by D'Herbelot: "Scheikh des plus considérés parmi les Musulmans. On le cite au sujet d'un passage du chapitre Enfathar de l'Alcoran (lxxxii.), où Dieu est introduit faisant ce reproche aux hommes:*Qu'est-ce qui*

vous rend si orgueilleux contre votre maître qui vous fait tant de biens? (v. 6). Ce Scheikh disait: *Quand Dieu me fera ce reproche, je lui repondrai: Le sont ces biens et ces graces mêmes que vous me faites, qui me rendent si superbe.*" As Sheykh 'Attār lived about A.H. 600, Mansūr must have died about A.H. 400 (A.D. 1020). He is mentioned in No. 51, p. 68, of the *Nafahātu-'l-Uns*.

14. Khayru 'n nāsi, men yenfa'u 'n nāsa.—Arabic Proverb.

15. Khayru 'l kelāmi, qasiruhu 'l mufīdu.—Arabic Proverb.

16. *Thevr* is the name of a tribe of Arabians, and of two hills, one at Mekka, the other at Medīna; but the explanation of the term "*a Thevr* or *Sevr veil*" I have not met with.

CHAPTER IV

Shemsu-'d-Dīn Tebrīzī, Muhammed son of 'Alī, son of Melik-dād.

1.

SHEMSU-'D-DĪN of Tebrīz was surnamed the Sultan of Mendicants, the Mystery of God upon earth, the Perfect in word and deed. Some had styled him the Flier, because he travelled about so much; and others spoke of him as the Perfect One of Tebrīz.

He went about seeking for instruction, human and spiritual. He had visited many of the chief spiritual teachers of the world; but he had found none equal to himself. The teachers of all lands became, therefore, pupils and disciples to him.

He was always in quest of the beloved object of the soul (God). His corporeal frame he habited in coarsest felt, shrouding his eminent greatness from all eyes in what are really the jewelled robes of spirituality.

At Damascus it was, where he was then studying, that he first saw Jelālu-'d-Dīn by chance in a crowded marketplace; but Jelāl, who was at that time a student also, avoided him.

Ultimately, he was led to Qonya in Jelāl's traces, and first arrived there at dawn, on Saturday, the twenty-sixth of Jumāda-'l-ākhir, A.H. 642 (28th November, A.D. 1244), Jelāl being then professor at four colleges there. They met as is related in a former chapter (chap. III. Nos. 8, 9).

At the end of three months' seclusion together, passed in religious, scientific, and spiritual disquisitions and investigations, Shemsu-'d-Dīn became satisfied that he had never met Jelāl's equal.

2.

When Shemsu-'d-Dīn was quite worn out by a series of divine manifestations and the consequent ecstasies, he used to break away, hide himself, and work as a day-labourer at the water-wheels of the Damascus gardens, until his equanimity would be restored. Then he would return to his studies and meditations.

In his supplications to God, he was constantly inquiring whether there was not in either world, corporeal and spiritual, one other saint who could bear him company. In answer thereto, there came at length from the unseen world the answer, that the one holy man of the whole universe who could bear him company was the Lord Jelālu-'d-Dīn of Rome.

On receiving this answer, he set out at once from Damascus, and went in quest of his object to the land of Rome (Asia Minor).

3.

Chelebī Emīr 'Ārif related that his father, Sultan Veled, told him that one day, as a trial and test, Shemsu-'d-Dīn requested Jelāl to make him a present of a slave. Jelāl instantly went and fetched his own wife, Kirā Khātūn, who was as extremely beautiful as virtuous and saintlike, offering her to him.

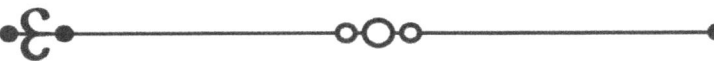

To this act of renunciation Shemsu-'d-Dīn replied: "She is my most esteemed sister. What I want is a youth to wait on me." Jelāl thereupon produced his own son, Sultan Veled, who, he said, would be proud to carry the shoes of Shems, placing them before him for use when required for a walk abroad. Again Shems objected: "He is as my son. But, perhaps, you will supply me with some wine. I am accustomed to drink it, and am not comfortable without it."

Jelāl now took a pitcher, went himself to the Jews' ward of the city, and returned with it full of wine, which he set before Shems.

"I now saw," continued Sultan Veled in his recital, "that Shemsu-'d-Dīn, uttering an intense cry, rent his garment, bowed down to Jelāl's feet, lost in wondering admiration at this implicit compliance with the behests of a teacher, and then said: 'By the truth of the First, who had no beginning, the Last, who will have no end, there never has been, from the commencement of creation, and there never, until the end of time, will be, in the universe of substance, a lord and master, heart-captivating and Muhammed-like, as thou art.'"

He now bowed down again, declared himself a disciple to Jelāl, and added: "I have tested and tried to the utmost the patient long-suffering of our Lord; and I have found his greatness of heart to be totally unlimited by any bounds."

4.

Jelāl is reported to have said: "When Shemsu-'d-Dīn first came, and I felt a mighty spark of love for him lighted up in my heart,

he took upon himself to command me in the most despotic and peremptory manner.

"'Study,' said he, 'the writings of thy father.' For a while I studied nothing else. 'Keep silent, and speak to no one.' I ceased from all intercourse with my fellows.

"My words were, however, the food of my disciples; my thoughts were the nectar of my pupils. They hungered and thirsted. Thence, ill feelings were engendered amongst them, and a blight fell upon my teacher.

"He came to me another day as I was, by his command, studying the writings of my father. Thrice he called out to me: 'Study them not.' From his sacred features the effulgence of spiritual wisdom streamed. I laid down the book, and never since have I opened it."

5.

Jelāl is said to have related that Shemsu-'d-Dīn forbade him to study any more the writings of his father, Bahā Veled, and that he punctually obeyed the injunction.

But one night he dreamt that he was in company with a number of friends, who were all studying and discussing with him those very writings of Bahā Veled.

As he woke from his dream, Shems was entering the room with a severe look. Addressing Jelāl, he asked: "How hast thou dared to study that book again?" Jelāl protested that, since his prohibition, he had never once opened his father's works.

"Yes," retorted Shems, "there is a study by reading, and there is also a study by contemplating. Dreams are but the shadows of our waking thoughts. Hadst thou not occupied thy thoughts with those writings, thou wouldst not have dreamt about them."

"From that time forward," remarked Jelāl, "I never again busied myself with my father's writings, so long as Shemsu-'d-Dīn remained alive."

6.

Jelāl is related to have informed his disciples that Shemsu-'d-Dīn was a scholar in every science known to man, and also a great alchemist; but that he had renounced them all, to devote himself to the study and contemplation of the mysteries of divine love.

7.

Shemsu-'d-Dīn was one day sitting with his disciples, when the public executioner passed by. Shems remarked to those around him: "There goes one of God's saints."

The disciples knew the man, and told Shems that he was the common headsman. Shems replied: "True! In the exercise of his calling, he put to death a man of God, whose soul he thus released from the bondage of the body.

As a recompense for this kind act of his, the saint bequeathed to him his own saintship."

On the following day the executioner relinquished his office, vowed repentance, came to Shemsu-'d-Dīn, made his bow, and professed himself a disciple.

8.

Sheykh Husāmu-'d-Dīn was originally a young man who showed great respect and humility towards Shemsu-'d-Dīn, to whom he rendered services of every kind.

One day Shems said to him: "Husām, this is not the way. Religion is a question of money. Give me some coin, and offer your services to the Lord; so, peradventure, thou mayest rise in our order."

Husām at once went forth to his own house, collected all his own valuables and money, with his wife's jewels, and all the provisions of the house, brought them to Shems, and laid them at his feet. He furthermore sold a vineyard and country-seat he possessed, bringing their price also to his teacher, and thanking him for having taught him a duty, as also for having deigned to accept so insignificant a trifle from his hand.

"Yes, Husām," said Shems, "it is to be hoped that, with God's grace, and the prayers of the saints, thou wilt henceforth attain to such a station, as to be the envy of the most perfect men of God, and be bowed down to by the *Brethren of Sincerity*. It is true that God's saints are not in want of anything, being independent of both worlds. But, at the outset, there is no other way to test the sincerity of one we love, and the affection of a friend, than to call upon him to sacrifice his worldly possessions. The next step is, to

summon him to give up all that is not his God. No disciple who wishes to rise, has ever made progress by following his own devices. Advancement is earned by rendering service, and by spending in God's cause. Every pupil who sacrifices possessions at the call of his teacher, would also lay down his life, if needs were. No lover of God can retain both mammon and religion."

Shems then restored to Husām the whole of his goods, keeping back only one piece of silver. Nine times as much more did he bestow upon Husām from first to last; and, as the results of all things are in God's hands, so did Husām at length become the ruler of God's saints, and Jelāl made him the keeper of God's treasury. He it was who wrote down the twenty-four thousand six hundred and sixty couplets contained in the six books of the Mesnevī.

9.

Shemsu-'d-Dīn left Qonya, at the end of his first visit, on Thursday, the twenty-first day of the month of Shawwal, A.H. 643 (14th March, A.D. 1246), after a stay of about sixteen months.

He returned to Damascus; and his departure left Jelāl in a state of great uneasiness and excitement. (Compare a conflicting date given in No. 13, further on.)

10.

Shemsu-'d-Dīn was one day at Bagdād, and entered one of the palaces there. A eunuch who saw him enter, without being himself visible, made a sign to a slave to go and drive away the mendicant.

The slave drew his sword, and raised it to strike; but his arm withered, and fell palsied.

The eunuch then motioned to another slave to execute the commission; and he, too, became similarly incapacitated.

Shems then went away of himself, and none dared to pursue him. Two days later, the eunuch died also.

11.

Jelāl's father, Bahā Veled, had a disciple, who, for some reason, gave offence to Shemsu-'d-Dīn; the latter, in punishment, inflicted a deafness on both the disciple's ears.

After a time, Shems pardoned the offender, and restored his hearing. But the man bore him a grudge in his heart, nevertheless. One day, Shems said to him: "Friend, I have pardoned thee; wherefore art thou still cast down? Be comforted." Notwithstanding this, his rancour remained.

One day, however, he met Shems in the midst of a market. Suddenly, he felt a new faith glow within him, and he shouted out: "There is no god save God; Shemsu-'d-Dīn is the apostle of God."

The market-people, on this, raised a great hubbub, and wished to kill him. One of them came forward to cut him down; but Shems

uttered so terrific a shout, that the man at once fell down dead. The rest of the market-people bowed, and submitted.

Shems now took the disciple by the hand, and led him away, remarking to him: "My good friend; my name is Muhammed. Thou shouldest have shouted: 'Muhammed is the apostle of God.' The rabble will not take gold that is not coined."

12.

One beautiful moonlight night, Jelāl and Shems were together on the terraced roof of the college, and all the inhabitants of Qonya were sleeping on their housetops.

Shems remarked: "See all these poor creatures! They are dead to every sense of their Creator on this beautiful night of God's decree. Wilt thou not, Jelāl, of thy infinite compassion, wake them up, and let them gain a share in the shower of blessings of this night?"

Thus appealed to, Jelāl faced toward Mekka, and offered up this prayer to God: "O Thou Lord of heaven, and of earth, for the love of Thy servant Shemsu-'d-Dīn, vouchsafe wakefulness to this people."

Immediately a black cloud gathered from the unseen world. Thunders and lightnings burst forth; and so heavy a rain fell, that all the sleepers, catching up what clothing they could find, quickly took refuge in their houses below. Shems smiled at the saintly joke, and was greatly amused.

When daylight dawned, the disciples gathered round, numerous as the raindrops of that shower; and Shems related to them the story, with the following remarks:—

"Hitherto, all the prophets and saints have ever sought to hide from vulgar eyes the miraculous powers they have possessed, so that none should be aware of the fact. But now, our Lord and Master, Jelāl, has been so successful in secretly following up the path of mystic love, that his miraculous powers have hitherto escaped the searching eyes of even the chiefest of God's elect, even as it hath been said: 'Verily, God hath saints of whom no man knoweth.'"

13.

Kimiyā Khātūn, the wife of Shemsu-'d-Dīn, was a very beautiful, and also a very virtuous, woman. One day, however, it so happened that, without his permission or knowledge, the grandmother of Sultan Veled, and her attendant ladies, took Kimiyā with them for an outing to the vineyards of the city.

As chance would have it, Shems came home while she was still away. He asked for her, and was informed where she had gone, and with whom. He was exceedingly annoyed at her absence.

Kimiyā had scarcely returned home, ere she began to feel unwell. Her limbs stiffened like dry firewood, and became motionless. She continued screaming and moaning for three days, and then gave up the ghost, in the month of Sha'bān, A.H.644 (December, A.D. 1246. But compare a conflicting date given in No. 9, further back.)

14.

It is related that, a second time, Shems and Jelāl shut themselves up for a whole six months in Jelāl's room at the college, without partaking of meat or drink, and without the entrance of a single individual to interrupt them, or either of them coming forth, Sultan Veled and one other disciple alone excepted.

15.

Shemsu-'d-Dīn was extremely bitter in his preachings and lectures to the learned auditory who used to gather around him in Qonya. He likened them to oxen and asses. He reproached them with being further than ever astray from the path of living love, and taxed them with the presumption of supposing themselves the equals of Bāyezīd of Bestām.

He once went to Erzen-of-Rome (Erzrūm), the prince of which city had a son so extremely stupid, though very handsome, that he could be taught nothing, or next thereto.

Shems let no one know who or what he was; but opened a school for children. Inquiries were made by the prince, and Shems undertook to instruct the child, and enable him, in one month, to recite the whole Qur'ān by heart.

He kept his promise. The young prince acquired, further, during the same period, a beautiful handwriting, and sundry other accomplishments.

It began to be suspected, now, that he was a saint in disguise. He therefore quietly slipped away from that city.

16.

There is a tradition that Jelāl one day called his son Sultan Veled, gave him a large sum of money, and bade him go, with a suite of the disciples, to Damascus, and request Shems to return to Qonya.

Jelāl told his son that he would find Shems in a certain inn, playing at backgammon with a young Firengī (European, Frank), also one of God's saints. Sultan Veled went, found Shems exactly so occupied, and brought him back to Qonya, the Firengī youth returning to his own country, there to preach Jelāl's doctrines, as his vicar.

Sultan Veled walked the whole way from Damascus to Qonya, at the stirrup-side of Shems, as a groom walks by the side of a prince's charger. The whole city went forth to receive them. Jelāl and Shems embraced each other. Jelāl became more than ever devoted to his friend; and his disciples resented his neglect of them, as they had done before. Not long afterwards, the dolorous event occurred that terminated the life of Shemsu-'d-Dīn.

17.

The Vazīr of Qonya had built a college. On its completion, he gave a great entertainment, in the college, of religious music and dancing, all the learned men of the city being present.

The Qur'ān was first recited in its entirety; after which, the holy waltzing began. The Vazīr and Shemsu-'d-Dīn both joined in the dance. Several times they came into collision; or, the Vazīr's skirt swept against Shems's person, as he observed no caution in his gyrations.

Jelāl expressed great indignation at this want of courtesy and reverence for his guest and friend. He took Shems by the hand, to lead him away. The grandees present essayed to appease him, but their entreaties were of no avail. The police of the Sultan were therefore sent for; and when they arrived, they instantly seized Shems, led him forth a prisoner with every mark of indignity, and put him to death without further inquiry or formality.

18.

Chelebī Emīr 'Ārif related, as informed by his mother, Fātima Khātūn, that when Shemsu-'d-Dīn was thus made a martyr, his executioners threw his corpse down a well.

Sultan Veled saw Shems in a dream, and was informed by him where the body would be found. Sultan Veled went therefore at midnight with some friends, recovered the corpse, washed it, and privately buried it in the college grounds, by the side of the founder.

19.

Forty days after the disappearance of Shemsu-'d-Dīn, Jelāl, wishing to appease his own sorrow, and quell the mutinous spirit that had broken out among the disciples, appointed Husāmu-'d-Dīn his local deputy, and set out to seek Shems at Damascus for the third time. All the learned men of Syria became his disciples, and he was absent about a year, more or less.

The Sultan and the nobles grew impatient at this long absence, and wrote him an urgent petition, begging him to return to Qonya. With this request he complied.

Naturally, he had failed to find Shemsu-'d-Dīn in the flesh at Damascus; but he had found within himself what was still greater. He went to the lodging of Shems, and wrote on the door, with red ink: "This is the station of the beloved one of Elias, on whom be peace!"

It is said that the body of Shemsu-'d-Dīn disappeared, and that he was buried by the side of Jelāl's father, Sultan Bahā Veled the Elder.

CHAPTER V

Sheykh Salāhu-'d-Dīn Ferīdūn,(1) surnamed Zer-Kūb (Goldbeater).

1.

SHEYKH SALĀHU-'D-DĪN was originally a fellow-disciple with Jelāl, as pupils to Seyyid Burhānu-'d-Dīn. He afterwards became a goldbeater, as his parents were poor.

After a while, when Jelāl's reputation became great, Salāh went and paid him his respects. Jelāl knew how highly Burhān had esteemed Salāh, when his pupil. He therefore received him in a very friendly manner, and their intercourse became warmly renewed.

One day, after the murder of Shemsu-'d-Dīn, and the return of Jelāl from Damascus, he sent for Salāh, and appointed him his own assistant in the government and instruction of the disciples, presenting him also to the king in that capacity.

2.

Jelāl's first royal protector, 'Alā'u-'d-Dīn Keyqubād, was now dead, and his son, Gayāsu-'d-Dīn Key-Khusrev, reigned in his stead.

The monarch one day made a feast in the vineyards, and went forth into the fields for a walk, alone. He picked up a young snake, carried it indoors, placed it in a gold box, sealed this up, and then rejoined his courtiers.

To those attendants the king exhibited the sealed packet, as having just then been privately received from the Qaysar (2) of Constantinople with a message to this effect: "If your religion of Islām be the true faith, some one of your wise men will be able to see into this packet without breaking its seals, and to tell what it contains."

The king then called upon his ministers to prove their loyalty to him, and their faithfulness to their religion, by solving this riddle. None of them was able.

The packet was now sent round in succession to all the eminent teachers and theologians of the city; but none could unravel the enigma.

At last it was brought to Jelāl, as Sheykh Ferīdūn and he were sitting together. Jelāl invited Ferīdūn to tell them the contents of the packet; and he immediately replied: "It is not a dignified act in the king to imprison a young snake in a gold box, sealing this up as a packet, and then tempting his courtiers, ministers, and learned men with a false pretence. A saint, however, knows not only the solution of so paltry a trick as this, but is also aware of every thought in the king's heart, and every secret of earth and heaven."

When this answer was reported to the king, he came to the college, and professed himself a disciple, remarking: "If the disciples of Shemsu-'d-Dīn possess such power, and work such miracles, how great must have been the sanctity of the murdered martyr."

Ferīdūn acted for ten years as assistant to Jelāl.

3.

Fātima, the daughter of Sheykh Salāhu-'d-Dīn Ferīdūn, was married to Sultan Veled, Jelāl's son. Jelāl used to teach her to read the Qur'ān and other books.

Jelāl used to call Fātima his *right eye;* her sister Hediyya, *his left eye;* and their mother, Latīfa Khātūn, *the personification of God's grace.*

When Fātima's marriage was solemnised, all the angels of heaven were present, and wished the young couple all happiness.

She was a saint, and continually worked miracles. She fasted by day and watched by night, tasting food only once in three days. She was very charitable to the poor, the orphans, and the widows, distributing to them food and raiment.

Sheykh Ferīdūn died on New Year's Day, A.H. 657 (28th December, A.D. 1258).

Footnotes

1. Saladin of European writings. The words mean: *the Fitness of the Religion* (of Islām).

2. The Muslim world knows but one *Qaysar* (Cæsar), the Emperor of Rome (Old or New), which title is now borne by the Emperor of Austria.

CHAPTER VI

Chelebī Husāmu-'l-Haqqi-wa-'d-Dīn, Hasan, son of Muhammed, son of Hasan, son of Akhī-Turk, (1) related to Esh-Sheykhu-'l-Mukerrem. (2)

1.

ON the death of Sheykh Ferīdūn, Chelebī Husāmu-'d-Dīn was appointed by Jelāl his assistant in place of the deceased saint. For another ten years these two spiritual friends worked together in perfect unity as Superior and Assistant. Husām was surnamed "the Juneyd and the Bāyezīd (3) of the age," "the Key of the Treasuries of God's throne," "the Trustee of the Treasures on earth," and "God's next Friend in the World."

2.

Husām once made his obeisance to Jelāl, and related to him that, when the disciples recited the poetry of the Mesnevī, and became entranced, he had himself seen a company of invisible ones, armed with clubs and scimitars, keeping guard over them. If any one did not listen to those sacred words with reverence and believing, the clubs and swords were brought into play, and he was hurled into the pit of hell-fire. Jelāl confirmed, as being a fact, all Husām had related.

3.

Husāmu-'d-Dīn was very eloquent, pious, and God-fearing. He would never use the water, even, of the college, for drink or for ablutions; but always brought his water from his own home for

those purposes. He distributed, to the very last farthing, the whole of the revenues of the college among the disciples.

4.

Sultan Veled and his friends went one day to Husām's garden. Some of the disciples felt a desire to eat of some honey, but had said nothing on the subject. Husām read their thoughts. He therefore ordered his gardener to bring some new honeycomb from a certain hive. More, and more, and still more comb was brought, until all were satisfied; still, the hive was yet full. When they left his garden, Husām sent the hive with them; and for a long time it supplied all their wants.

5.

A severe drought afflicted Qonya and its environs. Prayers for rain were publicly offered without avail.

Recourse was now had to Husāmu-'d-Dīn, who was begged to intercede for the people, and to pray for rain.

He first went to Jelāl's tomb, there performed his devotions to God, and then put up the prayer for rain, his disciples weeping as they chanted "Amen."

Clouds now began to collect and lower; shortly after which an abundance of rain was vouchsafed.

6.

Not only were all the revenues of the college, arising from its endowments, committed by Jelāl to the sole administration of

Husām, but, whatever gifts and contributions were offered by princes and friends, in money or in kind, they were all consigned to his care, to augment the resources of the general fund. Jelāl's family, and also his son, though often pinched, fared as the disciples.

7.

The disciples were both surprised and scandalised, at one time, by Husām's publicly speaking very much in praise of certain individuals who bore an extremely bad character, while he disparaged certain others who were noted for their pious lives.

They complained to Jelāl; but he confirmed what Husām had said, and remarked to them: "God looks only to man's heart. Those seemingly lewd fellows are really God-loving saints, while those outwardly pious livers are merely inward hypocrites."

8.

One day Husām was lecturing. Suddenly he beckoned to one of the disciples, and told him to go with all speed to the royal palace, ask to see the queen, give her his greeting, and say to her: "Instantly quit this apartment thou art in, if thou wouldest avoid impending destruction, the result of God's decree."

The queen believed his word, and at once removed to another part of the palace. The apartment was speedily stripped of its furniture; and scarcely had the last loads been removed, when, with a loud crash, the building fell in. Her faith in his miraculous power was thenceforward increased a hundredfold.

9.

A certain Sheykh died at Qonya, who was rector of two different colleges. The prince who was the trustee of both, elected to nominate Husāmu-'d-Dīn as rector of one of them; and a great entertainment was prepared by the prince for the occasion.

Jelāl was informed of the arrangement, and he expressed the intention to bear himself Husām's carpet to his new college, and himself spreading it for Husām in his new seat.

A certain brawler, a kinsman of Husām's, Akhī Ahmed by name, was of the company; and he had felt nettled at Husām's appointment. He came forward, snatched away Husām's carpet, gave it to one of his companions to cast out of the building, and exclaimed: "We will not suffer this fellow to be installed here as Sheykh."

Great confusion ensued. Several nobles of the Akhī clan, who were present, drew their swords and knives, a scene of blood appearing to be about to commence.

Jelāl now addressed the crowd, reproaching them for such behaviour. He told them that their family and college would not prosper, but that the Mevlevi order, founded by himself, and his lineal posterity would go on ever steadily increasing. He then related the following anecdote:—

"A certain Sheykh from Samarqand, Abū-'l-Lays by name, went on his travels for about twenty years, with a view to study, partly

at Mekka. At length he set out on his return home, whither his reputation, as well as numerous disciples, had preceded him.

"Arrived at the outskirts of his native place, he went to the riverside to perform an ablution. There he found a number of women, occupied with laundry work. From among these, one old woman advanced, looked at him attentively, and then exclaimed: 'Why, if here isn't our little Abū-'l-Lays come back again! Go quickly, girls, and carry the news to our family.'

"The Sheykh returned forthwith to his party of fellow-travellers, and gave orders for their beasts to be at once reloaded for an immediate return to Damascus. On being questioned as to his reason for this sudden change of intention he answered: 'My people still think of me as "*little Abū-'l-Lays*," and will treat me with familiar indignity accordingly, esteeming me of small account, and thereby committing a grievous sin; for it is an incumbent duty on all to honour the learned and the wise. To respect them is to show reverence to the apostle of God, and to revere him is to serve the Creator.'

"Now, the truth was that, when a child, his father had always called him 'little Abū-'l-Lays.' But strangers would not so understand that term of endearment; they would think it one of too free and easy familiarity, and as likely to draw down on the city and its inhabitants the divine displeasure. It was not consistent with true affection to allow the possibility of such a visitation to occur."

Having delivered himself of this constructive reprimand, Jelāl left the college barefoot, and in high dudgeon. The chief people came

after him to intercede, but he would not be pacified. Their intervention was declined, and he refused to be reconciled with the broiler, Akhī Ahmed. He would not consent to go near that offender, who died soon afterwards; though most of his sons, relatives, and even his fellow-revellers, became disciples of Jelāl's.

The Sultan would have caused him to be put to death at once; but Jelāl would not permit that.

Akhī Ahmed was never again allowed to show himself at any public reception, and was shunned by all, like the wandering Jew.

Eventually, Husāmu-'d-Dīn was appointed rector of both the colleges in question; and Ahmed's son, Akhī 'Alī, was a disciple of Sultan Veled.

10.

Jelālu-'d-Dīn was of the school of Abū-Hanīfa; but Husām belonged to that of Shāfi'ī. (4) He thought of joining the Hanefī school, out of deference to his teacher. Jelāl, however, recommended him to remain what he had always been, and to strive to inculcate to all the doctrine of divine love, as set forth by Jelāl.

11.

After Jelāl's death, his widow, Kirā Khātūn, suggested to her stepson, Sultan Veled Bahā'u-'d-Dīn, that he ought to have succeeded his father as Rector of the fraternity, and not Husain.

Sultan Veled answered that it had been his father's bequest that Husain should succeed, that he himself had sworn the oath of fealty to Husām, and that Husām was now become a kind of spiritual beehive, through the incessant and multitudinous visitations of angelic ministers sent to him with messages from on high.

12.

Husāmu-'d-Dīn had a gardener, whose name was Sheykh Muhammed. About four years after Jelāl's death, Husām had reason to reprimand the gardener, who took offence at this, and went away to another garden, resolved never to return to Husām's service.

As he sat reflecting, he fell asleep. In his dreams he saw Jelāl coming towards him, with an executioner by his side, who held up an axe. Jelāl ordered the executioner to cut off Muhammed's head, as the punishment for his having offended Husain.

This was done; and Muhammed saw his own head fall off, and his own blood flow. He knew that he was dead.

After a while he saw Jelāl return, pick up Muhammed's decapitated head, place it in proper junction with the neck of the corpse, and utter the exclamation: "In the name of God, with God, from God, and to God." Muhammed saw himself instantly alive again, felt very penitent, threw himself at Jelāl's feet, and cried out piteously.

He now awoke and arose. No one was in sight. All traces of blood had vanished, and no sign of a wound was discernible on his neck. In all speed he returned to Husām's garden, and resumed his work with alacrity.

But now he saw Husain approaching, who said to him:

"Well, Sheykh Muhammed! Until Jelālu-'d-Dīn chastised thee, thou wert no Muslim, and wert given over to stiffneckedness. Had not I interceded for thee, thou hadst been dead to all eternity, shut out from every hope of heaven."

Muhammed protested his sincere repentance, became a dervish, and professed himself a disciple.

13.

When Husāmu-'d-Dīn had faithfully executed for ten years, as a just and wise steward, all his duties as successor to Jelālu-'d-Dīn, he one day went, with his companions and disciples, to visit the shrine of his predecessor.

As he drew near to the mausoleum, information was brought to him that the gilt crescent surmounting the cupola had fallen down.

On the moment, Husām felt himself to be stricken. He asked for an examination of dates to be made, and found that ten years previously Jelāl had departed this life. He therefore said to those around him: "Lead me back home. The time for my dissolution is at hand."

He was conducted to his chamber, where, a few days later, on Thursday, the twenty-second of Sha'bān, in the year A.H. 683 (4th November, A.D. 1284), he breathed his last exactly at the time when the gilt crescent was replaced over Jelāl's tomb, and the works brought to a close.

14.

Shortly after the death of Husāmu-'d-Dīn, the widow of Jelāl, Kirā Khātūn, too, departed this life, and was buried by the side of her husband.

As her corpse was being borne towards its last resting-place, the procession passed through one of the gates of the town. Here, the bearers found themselves arrested by some unseen power, so that they could not move, hand or foot. This singular effect lasted for about half an hour.

Her stepson, Sultan Veled, with the other mourners, struck up a hymn, and commenced a holy dance. Soon after this, the bearers recovered the use of their limbs, and found themselves able to proceed. All now went well, and the interment was completed.

That same night, a holy man of the fraternity saw Kirā Khātūn in heaven near to her husband. (5) He inquired of her concerning the arrestation of the funeral. She informed him thus: "The day previous, a man and a woman had been stoned to death at that gate for the sin of adultery. I took compassion on them, interceded for their forgiveness, and obtained for them admittance to paradise. My preoccupation in their cause was the reason of the delay met with by the funeral procession."

15.

One day, while Jelāl was yet living, Satan appeared in person to Husāmu-'d-Dīn, and complained bitterly of the torments inflicted on him by the continuous pious exercises of Jelāl. He said that such was his deep reverence for Jelāl and his followers, that he dared not attempt to seduce one of them; and that, had he known that, of the seed of Adam, so holy a race of men were to spring, he never would have tempted the father of mankind. He further added: "I entertain a hope that the kindness of heart of his sons will lead them to intercede with Jelāl for me, and so obtain my eventual release and salvation."

Husām related this occurrence to Jelāl, who smiled, and said: "There is reason to hope that he need not despair. God forbid that he should despair!"

16.

Whenever the grandees of Qonya entertained a desire to have an audience of the Sheykh Shemsu-'d-Dīn of Tebrīz, during his lifetime, they used to request Husām to beg Jelāl to intercede for them with Shems, and so obtain for them the desired interview.

Jelāl and Husām used to tax those nobles for this favour, according to their means and circumstances.

On one occasion the Grand Vazīr solicited an audience, and was taxed at forty thousand pieces of silver; which, after much chaffering, was reduced to thirty thousand.

At his audience with Shems, the Vazīr was so charmed with the mysteries revealed to him, that, on his return therefrom, he voluntarily sent the ten thousand pieces of silver to Husām, which had been abated from the sum originally fixed.

These monies were always expended by Husām, as he saw fit, in relieving the necessities of the holy community, and the families of Jelāl, the Goldbeater, and their various dependants.

Footnotes

1. I have not met with any notice of Akhī-Turk.

2. *The Honoured Elder;* by which Abū-Bekr is probably intended; but see a note to the Preface of the Mesnevī.

3. Juneyd and Bāyezīd of Bestām were two great doctors of mysticism; the latter died in A.H. 234 or 261 (A.D. 848 or 874), and the former in A.H. 297-8 (A.D. 909-10).

4. These are two of the four orthodox schools of Islām; they differ in certain details. There are reputed to be seventy-two schismatic or heretical sects.

5. This anecdote directly contradicts the foolish idea, so common in Europe, that, in the religious system of Islām, women are held to have no souls, and no hope of paradise.

CHAPTER VII

The Sultan of them who attain to the Truth, in whom are manifested the mysteries of Positive Knowledge, Bahā'u-'l-Haqqiwa-'d-Dīn, (1) El Veled.

1.

WHILE Sultan Veled was yet a child, his father, Jelālu-'d-Dīn, was once discoursing on the miracle of the rod of Moses, which swallowed up the rods and other engines of Pharaoh's magicians, related to have been in such quantities as to form seventy camel-loads, and yet that staff became no thicker or longer than before.

Turning to Sultan Veled, his father asked how this could be, and to what it could be likened for the sake of illustration.

The child at once replied: "In a very dark night, if a lighted taper be brought into a large room or hall, it instantly devours all the darkness, and yet remains a little taper."

Jelāl jumped up from his seat, ran to his son, took the child to his bosom, kissed him with effusion, and then said: "May God bless thee, my child! Verily, thou hast strung a pearl of the very first water on the string of illustration."

2.

Sultan Veled's elder brother, 'Alā'u-'d-Dīn, was killed in the tumult for which the police authorities of Qonya put to death the Sheykh Shemsu-'d-Dīn of Tebrīz. Sultan Veled ruled the dervish community, in room of his father after the death of Husāmu-'d-Dīn), for many years (from A.H. 683 to 712, being twenty-nine lunar years). He composed three volumes of poetry in couplets, like the Mesnevī (hence styled *Mesneviyāt*, Mesnevian Poems), and a volume (*Dīwān*) of odes in the Arabian style, arranged in the alphabetical order of their rhymes.

3.

It is related that when Husāmu-'d-Dīn was in his last illness, Sultan Veled came to visit him. Finding the sickness was unto death, he began to wail and lament, asking what would become of himself after the removal of so dear a friend and so able a director.

Husām collected himself, and, leaning on Sultan Veled, sat up. He then addressed the latter thus: "Be of good cheer, and let not thy heart be dismayed through my departure in the body. In another form, I will ever be near thee still. Thou shalt never be in need of counsel from another. In all difficulties and troubles that may beset thee, I will always be present, and in the visions of the night will I solve every doubt, and direct thee in each matter, whether it relate to the spirit and religion, or whether it pertain to the flesh and mundane affairs. Whenever thou shalt receive counsel in this manner, know of a surety that it is I who suggest it to thee—it will be none other than I myself. I will show myself to thee in thy visions; and I will be thy counsel and thy guide."

Sultan Veled was the first who narrated his dreams in his poems. Seek them there; there shalt thou find them consigned.

4.

One day a great man asked Sultan Veled whether God ever speaks to His servant—man.

This inquirer had frequently had the idea to send an offering to Sultan Veled; but had hesitated between a gift of money and one of Indian muslins.

Sultan Veled answered his inquiry thus: "God does certainly speak to His servants. And as to the method by which He addresses then, I will relate to thee an anecdote."

"There was in Balkh a preacher, who was also one of God's most precious saints. He had many disciples, who loved him dearly. I heard him once say, during one of his discourses: 'Long hath God spoken to you in words; but you will not hearken to Him. This conduct is strangely improper on the part of obsequious servants. In God's name, therefore, I warn you that you ought to hearken to God's words, and yield obedience to His commands.'

"Just then, a dervish in the congregation stood up, and begged that some one would bestow on him a handkerchief.

"A merchant, who was seated in a corner of the mosque, thrice conceived the resolve to give the dervish a handkerchief; but thrice he failed to carry that design into effect.

"That merchant now rose, and, addressing the preacher, said: 'Sir, how does God speak to His servants? Pray explain this, that the method may be known unto us.'

"The preacher answered: 'For one handkerchief, God does not speak more than three times!'

"The merchant was petrified. He cried aloud, and cast himself at the feet of the preacher. What he had thrice resolved to do, and had not performed, he now carried out, giving a handkerchief to the dervish, and professing himself a disciple to the preacher."

"Now," added Sultan Veled, "I say unto thee, O grandee, do thou also hearken unto the words of God. Give the Indian handkerchiefs, and distribute 'also the money. When thou shalt have hearkened to the words of God, He will listen also to that which thou mayest say unto Him. All thou mayest ask of Him, God will give thee; and whatsoever thou seekest of Him, thou shalt find."

Forthwith that grandee became a sincere convert and disciple. Similar miraculous works of Sultan Veled are beyond all count.

5.

Sultan Veled died on Saturday, the tenth day of Rejeb, A.H. 712 (11th November, A.D. 1312). He had as many as a dozen children by his wife Fātima, daughter of the Sheykh Salāhu-'d-Dīn Ferīdūn, the Goldbeater; but they all died in infancy, immediately after birth, or ere they were six months old. At length, on a Monday, the eighth day of the month of Zū-'l-Qa'da, A.H. 670 (6th May, A.D. 1272), his son and successor, Chelebī Emīr 'Ārif, was born.

Soon after his birth, or when only a few months old, the Emīr 'Ārif, at the invitation of his grandfather, Jelālu-'d-Dīn, and in the hearing of a numerous circle of assembled friends, thrice pronounced, audibly and distinctly, God's great name. His

grandfather prophesied thence that he would be a very great saint, and would sit in the seat of his own successorship, after his father Sultan Veled. The Emīr 'Ārif lived about fifty years, surviving his father, however, but the short term of eight or nine summers.

Footnotes

1. The Beauty of the Truth and of the Religion (of Islām).

CHAPTER VIII

Chelebī Emīr 'Ārif, Jelālu-'d-Dīn.

(**NINETY** pages of the volume by Eflākī give more than two hundred anecdotes of the acts and miracles, of various kinds, of this illustrious grandson of Jelālu-'d-Dīn, the teacher and friend of the author, who vouches as an eyewitness for the truth and correctness of some of the narratives.

The Emīr 'Ārif passed the far greater portion of his life in travelling about to various cities in central and eastern Asia Minor, and north-western Persia, countries then subject to the great Khāns, descendants of Jengīz. He appears to have been of a more energetic or bellicose character than his father, and to have ruled with vigour during his short Rectorship.)

1.

On the last day but one of the period of the greater pilgrimage at Mekka, the eve of the Festival of Sacrifices, the ninth of the month of Zū-'l-Hijja, A.H. 717 (11th February, A.D. 1313), the Emīr 'Ārif, and the historian Eflākī, his disciple, were together at Sultāniyya, in the north of Persia, the new capital of the great western Mogul empire.

They were visiting at the convent of a certain Mevlevi dervish, named Sheykh Suhrāb, (1) with sundry of the friends and saints, all of whom were engaged in the study of different books, at about the hour of midday, excepting 'Ārif, who was enjoying a *siesta*.

Suddenly, 'Ārif raised his head, and gave one of his loud, awe-inspiring shouts, which caused all present to tremble. Without a word, however, he again composed himself to sleep.

When he at length fully roused himself, and finally woke up from his sleep, Sheykh Eflākī ventured to inquire what it was that had disturbed him.

He answered: "I had gone in the spirit to pay a visit to the tomb of my great-grandfather, when there I saw the two Mevlevī dervishes, Nāsiru-'d-Dīn and Shujā'u-'d-Dīn Chanāqī, who had seized each other by the collar, and were engaged in a violent dispute and struggle. I called out to them to desist; and two men, with one pious woman, being there present, saw me."

Eflākī at once made a note of this narrative, putting down the date and hour of the occurrence.

Some time afterwards, 'Ārif returned to the land of Rome, and went to the town of Lādik (*Laodicæa Combusta*, not far from Qonya); and there they met the above-named Nāsiru-'d-Dīn. In the presence of all the friends, 'Ārif asked Nāsir to relate to them the circumstances of his quarrel with Shujā'.

Nāsir replied: "On the eve of the Festival of Sacrifices, I was standing at the upper end of the mausoleum, when Shujā' came there, and committed an unseemly act, for which I reprehended him. He immediately collared me, and I him; when suddenly, from the direction of the feet of the holy Bahā Veled, the voice of 'Ārif was heard shouting to us, and made us tremble. In awe thereat, we immediately embraced each other, and bowed in reverence. That is all I know of the matter."

'Ārif then addressed Eflākī, and said: "Pray relate to our friends what thou knowest thereof, that they may be edified."

Eflākī now produced his memorandum-book, and showed the entry he had made, with the date. The friends marvelled at this, and rejoiced exceedingly, their spirits being refreshed with an influence from the invisible world.

'Ārif then said: "By the soul of my ancestor, I dislike exceedingly to make a display of any miraculous power. But, now and then, for the edification of my disciples, such scenes will slip out. Then Eflākī takes note thereof."

Such miracles are known by the names of "manifestations," and "ektasis of the spirit."

When Qonya was reached, three friends, one a lady, bore testimony to having seen 'Ārif at the tomb on that day, and to their having heard him shout.

2.

'Ārif's last journey was from Lārenda to Aq-Serāy (on the road to Qonya). In the latter place he remained about ten days; when, one night, he laid his head on his pillow, and wept bitterly, continuously moaning and sobbing in his sleep.

In the morning his friends inquired the cause. He said he had seen a strange dream. He was seated in a vaulted chamber, with

windows looking on to a garden as beautiful as paradise, with all kinds of flowering shrubs and fruit-bearing trees, beneath the shade of which the youths and maidens of heaven were walking and disporting themselves. Melodious voices were also heard. In one direction he noticed a flower-garden, and there he saw his grandfather, Jelālu-'d-Dīn. He wondered at his appearance; when lo, Jelāl looked towards him, and beckoned him to approach. On his drawing near, Jelāl asked him what had brought him there; and then added: "The time is come; the end of thy term. Thou must come to me."

It was from joy and delight at this kind invitation of his grandfather, that 'Ārif had wept and sobbed.

He then said: "It is time for me to make my journey to heaven,— to drink of the cup of God's might."

Two days later, they continued their journey towards Qonya, and 'Ārif showed some slight symptoms of indisposition.

These daily grew more severe. He reached Qonya. One morning he came out of his house, and stood in the gateway of his great-grandfather's mausoleum, silent, in the midst of his disciples. It was Friday, the last day of the month of Zū-'l-qa'da, A.H. 719 (13th January, A.D. 1320).

The orb of the sun rose like a disk of gold, careering over the azure vault from an impulse given to it by the bat of God's decree. It attained the altitude of a lance-length. 'Ārif contemplated it, and smiled. Shortly afterwards, he spoke as follows:

"I am tired of this lower world, and have no wish to remain beneath the sun, surrounded with dust and misery. The time is come for me to trample on the stars that encircle the pole, mounting beyond the sun, to occupy myself with the mysteries of the heavenly choir, and to be entirely delivered from the instabilities of this world of change."

His disciples burst into tears, and he continued—

"There is no remedy hereto, but to die. During life, my pleasure has been to journey and wander about, in outward space, and in inward self-exploration. For idle spirits come into the world of material forms to contemplate the marvels of the horizons, and the wonders of men's minds,—to acquire knowledge, and attain to certainty. Through the gravity of the body I have been impeded in the investigation, and I shall not be able to travel again. Let me, then, wend my way to the future state, for here below I have no real companion. My only anxiety is, to be with my father and grandfather. How long shall I be severed from them in this world of suffering? I long to behold my grandfather, and I will certainly depart."

He then cried aloud. After which he slowly returned to his chamber, and there continued to moan.

He managed to crawl, as well as he could, to the congregational service of worship of that Friday at noon. Thence he proceeded to the mausoleum, kissed the shrine, sang a hymn, performed a holy dance, and uttered ecstatic cries. He then laid himself down at full length on the floor, under which he is now buried, and said:

"Where the man falls, there let him be interred. Bury you the deposit of my corpse in this spot."

That day was as though the last judgment were at hand. A tempest arose; all creation, mortal and immortal, seemed to be groaning.

The day following, Saturday, the traces of his malady were but too visible in 'Ārif's features. He strove to battle with it, and to converse, as if he were in perfect health.

His sickness lasted about five and twenty days. On the twenty-second of Zū-'l-Hijja there was a violent shock of earthquake.

There was then in Qonya a certain saint, commonly known as *"the Student,"* a successor of the legist Ahmed. In his youth he had made himself a great reputation for learning, in all its branches. But, for forty years, he had been paralysed, and had never risen from his seat, summer or winter. He was well versed in all mysteries, and now began to say: "They are taking away the lamp of Qonya! Alas, the world will go to utter confusion! I, too, will follow after that holy man!"

Shocks followed after shocks of the earthquake; and 'Ārif exclaimed: "The hour of departure is at hand! See, the earth yawns for the mouthful it will make of my body. It shows signs of impatience for its food!"

He then asked: "Look! What birds are these that are come here?" His eyes remained fixed for a time on the angelic visions which he now saw. From time to time he would start, as though about to

fly. The assembled disciples, men and women, wept bitterly. But he again spoke, and said—

"Sheykhs, be not troubled! Even as my descent into this world was for the regulation of the affairs of your community, so is my existence of equal advantage to you, and I will at all times be with you, never absent from you. Even in the other world will I be with you. Here below, separation is a thing unavoidable. In the other world there is union without disrupture, and junction without a parting. Let me go without a pang. To outward appearance, I shall be absent; but in truth, I shall not be away from you. So long as a sword is in its sheath, it cuts not; but, when it shall be drawn, you shall see its effects. From this day forward, I dash my fist through the curtain that veils the invisible world; and my disciples shall hear the clash of the blows."

As he spake these words, his eldest son, Shāh-Zāda, and his own half-brother, Chelebī 'Ābid, entered the room. Sheykh Eflākī asked him what commands he had to give for them. 'Ārif replied: "They belong to the Lord, and have no longer a relation to me; He will take care of them."

Eflākī now asked: "And what are your wishes with respect to me, your most humble servant?" The answer was: "Do thou remain in the service of the mausoleum. Forsake it not. Go not elsewhere. That which I have commanded thee to do, as to collecting in writing all the memoirs of my ancestors and family, that do thou in all diligence until its completion. So mayest thou be approved of the Lord, and blessed by His saints."

All wept.

'Ārif now recited some verses; pronounced thrice the holy name of God, with a sigh; recited some more verses; and then, between the noon and afternoon hours of worship, having recited two short chapters of the Qur'ān, he departed, in peace and rejoicing, to the centre of his existence, on Tuesday, the twenty-fourth day of Zū-'l-Hijja, A.H. 719 (5th February, A.D. 1320). Unto God be all glory, now and for ever!

He was buried on the 25th, where he had himself indicated, by the side of his grandfather. His half-brother 'Ābid succeeded him.

Footnotes

1. Europeanised Armenians have made this into *Zohrab*, as their own family name.

CHAPTER IX

Genealogy of Jelālu-'d-Dīn, Rūmī.

ON his father's side, the remote ancestor of Jelālu-'d-Dīn, during Islāmic times, was Abū-Bekr, the dearest and most faithful friend of Muhammed the Arabian lawgiver, and his successor in the government of the community of Islām, as the first of the long line of Caliphs.

Like Muhammed himself, Abū-Bekr was of the tribe of Quraysh, which claims descent, through Ishmael, from Abraham, the chosen Friend of God, and Father of the faithful. The stem of Abū-Bekr's branch of the tribe unites with that of Muhammed in Murra, ancestor to Muhammed in the seventh degree, and to Abū-Bekr in the sixth.

Abū-Bekr was, furthermore, one of Mohammed's fathers-in-law, as his daughter 'Ā'isha was the Prophet's only virgin bride.

A son or grandson of Abū-Bekr is said to have been among the Arabian conquerors of Khurāsān during the caliphate of 'Uthmān (Osmān), about A.H. 25 (A.D. 647), and to have settled at Balkh (the capital of the ancient Bactria), where his family flourished until after the birth of Jelālu-'d-Dīn. (1)

At an uncertain period subsequent to A.H. 491 (A.D. 1097), a daughter of one of the Kh'ārezmian kings of Central Asia was given in marriage to Jelālu-'d-Dīn's great-great-grandfather, whose name is either not mentioned by Eflākī, or I have missed it. She gave birth to Jelāl's great-grandfather, Ahmed, surnamed El-

Khatībī (as being, apparently, a son or descendant, or a client, of a public preacher, Khatīb).

Nothing more is mentioned of Ahmed by Eflākī, than that he had a son Huseyn, surnamed Jelālu-'d-Dīn, who married a daughter of a certain Khurrem-Shāh, King of Khurāsān, and became grandfather, by her, to the author of the Mesnevī. His son, Mohammed, surnamed Bahā'u-'d-Dīn, styled Sultānu-'l-'Ulemā, and commonly known as Bahā'u-'d-Dīn Veled, or shorter as Bahā Veled, appears also to have married a lady, by whom he had three children, a daughter and two sons.

Bahā Veled's eldest child, his daughter, was married off, and remained at Balkh, when Bahā Veled, his mother, and two sons left it, a year or so before it was taken and devastated by Jengīz Khān in A.H. 608 (A.D. 1211). His elder son is not again mentioned by Eflākī after their departure from Balkh. Neither is the mother of his children once mentioned. But his own mother, the princess, was alive, and was still with him in about A.D. 1230; after which, she too is not again mentioned.

Bahā Veled's youngest child, his most celebrated son Mohammed, surnamed Jelālu-'d-Dīn, Mevlānā, Khudāvendgār, and Rūmī, the principal personage of these memoirs, the founder of the order of the Mevlevī dervishes, and author of the Mesnevī, had four children, three boys and a girl, by two wives. His eldest son was killed in the broil that caused the murder of his father's friend Shemsu-'d-Dīn of Tebrīz. His youngest son is not taken further notice of; but his daughter was married off to a local prince, and left Qonya.

His second son, and eventually his successor as Principal or Abbot of his order, was named Muhammed, and surnamed Bahā'u-'Dīn. He is commonly known as Sultan Veled.

Sultan Veled had six children, a boy and two girls by his wife Fātima, daughter of Sheykh Ferīdūn the Gold-beater, and three boys, of whom two were twins, by two slave women. The daughters married well, and all his sons, or three of them, succeeded him as Abbot, one after the other. The eldest was Mīr 'Ārif (Chelebī Emīr 'Ārif), the second was named 'Ābid, the third Zāhid, and the fourth Wāhid.

Chelebī Emīr 'Arif, the eldest, and Eflākī's patron, had two sons and a daughter. His eldest son, Emīr 'Ālim, surnamed Shāh-zāda, succeeded eventually to the primacy after his uncles. With him, Eflākī's memoir is brought to a close.

Such was the natural line of this dynasty of eminent men. But Eflākī has also given the links of a spiritual series, through whom the mysteries of the dervish doctrines were handed down to and in the line of Jelālu-'d-Dīn.

In the anecdote No. 79, of chapter III., the account is given of the manner in which the prophet Muhammed confided those mysteries to his cousin, son-in-law, and afterwards his fourth successor, as Caliph, 'Alī son of Abū-Tālib, the "Victorious Lion of God."

'Alī communicated the mysteries to the Imām Hasan of Basra, who died in A.H. 110 (A.D. 728); Hasan taught them to Habīb the Persian, (2) who confided them to Dāwūd of the tribe of

Tayyi',—Et-Tā'ī (mentioned by D'Herbelot, without a date, as Davud Al Thai; he died A.H. 165, A.D. 781).

Dāwūd transmitted them to Ma'rūf of Kerkh (who died A.H. 200, A.D. 815); he to Sirrī the merchant of damaged goods (Es-Saqatī?; died A.H. 253, A.D. 867); and he to the great Juneyd (who died in about A.H. 297—A.D. 909). Juneyd's spiritual pupil was Shiblī (died A.H. 334, A.D. 945) who taught Abu-'Amr Muhammed, son of Ibrāhīm Zajjāj (the Glazier), of Nīshāpūr (who died in A.H. 348—A.D. 959) and his pupil was Abū-Bekr, son of 'Abdu-'llāh, of Tūs, the Weaver, who taught Abū-Ahmed (Muhammed son of Muhammed, El-Gazālī (who died A.H. 504—A.D. 1110), and he committed those mysteries to Ahmed el-Khatībī, Jelāl's great-grandfather, who consigned them to the Imām Sarakhsī (who died in A.H. 571—A.D. 1175).

Sarakhsī was the spiritual teacher of Jelāl's father Bahā Veled, who taught the Seyyid Burhānu-'d-Dīn Termīzi, the instructor of Jelāl. He again passed on the tradition to Shemsu-'d-Dīn of Tebrīz, the teacher of Jelāl's son, Sultan Veled, who himself taught the Emīr 'Ārif.

At the same time that the mysteries were thus being gradually transmitted to Jelālu-'d-Dīn and his successors by these links, they were also being diffused in thousands of other channels, and are at this day widely diffused over the world of Islām, which daily boasts of its living saints and their miracles. These latter are perhaps not less veracious that those continually blazoned forth by the Church of Rome, and by its Eastern sisters. We, too, have our spiritualists. Credulity will never forsake mankind and

prodigies will never be lacking for the credulous to place faith in. There is much that is human in man, all the world over.

Footnotes

1. A genealogy is given in the Turkish preface to my copy of the Mesnevī, which traces the descent of Jelālu-'d-Dīn Mohammed from Abū-Bekr in ten degrees, as follows:—"Jelālu-'d-Dīn, son of Bahā'u-'d-Dīn, son of Huseyn, son of Ahmed, son of Mevdūd, son of Sābit (Thābit), son of Museyyeb, son of Mutahhar, son of Hammād, son of 'Abdu-'r-Rahmān, son of 'Abū-Bekr." Now, Abdu-'r-Rahmān, the eldest of all the sons of Abū-Bekr, died and was buried at Mekka in A.H. 53(A.D.672), and p. 133 Jelālu-'d-Dīn was born at Balkh in A.H. 604 (A.D. 1207). Between these two there are nine degrees of descent given, for a period of 535 years, or 66 years for each life after the birth of the next link. This alone suffices to show that the genealogy is not to be depended on. Supposing the names given to be true, many other links must be missing; as many, probably, as those given.

2. Habīb the Persian, a wealthy man, converted to Islam by one word from Hasan of Basra, whose devoted disciple he became. He died A.H. 106 (A.D. 724).

www.ingramcontent.com/pod-product-compliance
Lightning Source LLC
Chambersburg PA
CBHW031353040426
42444CB00005B/278